The WOODWORKER'S COMPLETE SHOP REFERENCE

POPULAR WOODWORKING BOOKS

CINCINNATI, OHIO
www.popularwoodworking.com

J. CHURCHILL

READ THIS IMPORTANT SAFETY NOTICE

To prevent accidents, keep safety in mind while you work. Use the safety guards installed on power equipment; they are for your protection. When working on power equipment, keep fingers away from saw blades, wear safety goggles to prevent injuries from flying wood chips and sawdust, wear headphones to protect your hearing, and consider installing a dust vacuum to reduce the amount of airborne sawdust in your woodshop. Don't wear loose clothing, such as neckties or shirts with loose sleeves, or jewelry, such as rings, necklaces or bracelets, when working on power equipment. Tie back long hair to prevent it from getting caught in your equipment. People who are sensitive to certain chemicals should check the chemical content of any product before using it. The authors and editors who compiled this book have tried to make the contents as accurate and correct as possible. Plans, illustrations, photographs and text have been carefully checked. All instructions, plans and projects should be carefully read, studied and understood before beginning construction. In some photos, power tool guards have been removed to more clearly show the operation being demonstrated. Always use all safety guards and attachments that come with your power tools. Due to the variability of local conditions, construction materials, skill levels, etc., neither the author nor Popular Woodworking Books assumes any responsibility for any accidents, injuries, damages or other losses incurred resulting from the material presented in this book. Prices listed for supplies and equipment were current at the time of publication and are subject to change. Glass shelving should have all edges polished and must be tempered. Untempered glass shelves may shatter and can cause serious bodily injury. Tempered shelves are very strong and if they break will just crumble, minimizing personal injury.

METRIC CONVERSION CHART

to convert	to	multiply by
Inches	Centimeters	2.54
Centimeters	Inches	0.4
Feet	Centimeters	30.5
Centimeters	Feet	0.03
Yards	Meters	0.9
Meters	Yards	1.1
Sq. Inches	Sq. Centimeters	6.45
Sq. Centimeters	Sq. Inches	0.16
Sq. Feet	Sq. Meters	0.09
Sq. Meters	Sq. Feet	10.8
Sq. Yards	Sq. Meters	0.8
Sq. Meters	Sq. Yards	1.2
Pounds	Kilograms	0.45
Kilograms	Pounds	2.2
Ounces	Grams	28.3
Grams	Ounces	0.035

The Woodworker's Complete Shop Reference. Copyright © 2003 by Jennifer Churchill. Manufactured in China. All rights reserved. No part of this book may be reproduced in any form or by any electronic or mechanical means, including information storage and retrieval systems, without permission in writing from the publisher, except by a reviewer, who may quote brief passages in a review. Published by Popular Woodworking Books, an imprint of F&W Publications, Inc., 4700 East Galbraith Road, Cincinnati, Ohio, 45236. First edition.

Visit our Web site at www.popularwoodworking.com for more information and resources for woodworkers.

Other fine Popular Woodworking Books are available from your local bookstore or direct from the publisher.

07   06   05   04   03   5   4   3   2   1

Library of Congress Cataloging-in-Publication Data
Churchill, J. (Jennifer)
  The woodworkers complete shop reference / by J. Churchill.--1st ed.
    p. cm.
Includes index.
  ISBN 1-55870-632-1 (pbk.; alk. paper)
  1. Woodwork. I. Woodworking tools. I. Title
  TT180.C49 2003
  684'.08--dc21
                    2003045966

ACQUISITIONS EDITOR: Jim Stack
EDITOR: Jennifer Ziegler
DESIGNER: Brian Roeth
LEAD PHOTOGRAPHY BY: Greg DeKraker
PRODUCTION COORDINATOR: Mark Griffin
TECHNICAL ILLUSTRATIONS BY: Len Churchill
PAGE LAYOUT ARTIST: Christine Long

This book is dedicated to the staff of Popular Woodworking,
who have been my teachers, my editors and my friends.

ABOUT THE AUTHOR

Jennifer Churchill lives in Hubbardston, Michigan. She is an admirer of men and women who have the gumption and skill to make things with their hands. Jennifer has worked with woodworkers for many years, as the publicity coordinator for the John C. Campbell Folk School in Brasstown, North Carolina, and as an editor for Popular Woodworking Books, where she first learned to fear the router and respect the table saw. She is currently an editor at the *Lansing State Journal* in Lansing, Michigan, and the publisher and editor of *West Michigan Woman* magazine.

ACKNOWLEDGEMENTS

Many thanks go to my acquisitions editor and friend, Jim Stack, who taught me how to keep all my fingers intact when using power tools.

Thanks to Sharon and Bud Datema for the use of their home, their woodshop, their time and their tools.

I would also like to thank and acknowledge the following: my editor, Jenny Ziegler, for her infinite patience; Michelle Cunningham, for encouraging me to write this book; my family for their support during this busy and hectic time; and many others who gave me encouragement and assistance, including Alex Cash, Pat and Liz Churchill, Charles Churchill, Karmen Datema, Greg DeKraker, Dave Folmsbee, Mary Lynne LeFere, Ryon List and Rhandi Riley.

Special thanks to the Public Museum of Grand Rapids, Blue Magruder at the Earthwatch Institute, Gary Halstead, the Renwick Gallery of the Smithsonian American Art Museum, Doug Roach of Lutz File & Tool Company, Todd Langston, David Smith, Herr Rausch, Andrew Glasgow of The Furniture Society, Neil Marko of Soss, the Hardwood Manufacturers Association, Ann Rockler Jackson, Carla Jackson-Tucker of Gibbs Smith Publisher, Sandra Morgan at the United States Department of Agriculture's Forest Products Laboratory and the National Hardwood Lumber Association.

Thanks also to Len Churchill, who, for the record, is no relation, but is a great woodworking illustrator and a great person to work with.

TABLE OF **contents**

CHAPTER ONE

① wood . . . 12

species, uses and characteristics

CHAPTER TWO

② hardware . . . 28

fasteners, knobs and brackets

CHAPTER THREE

③ shop math . . . 44

circles, squares and measurements

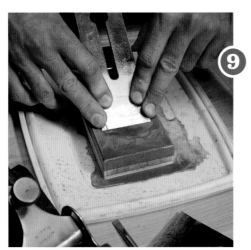

sidebars

> introduction

There are a lot of reference books out there, but they all seem to be a little overly detailed for the average woodworker's needs, with scientific charts and graphs. This shop reference will attempt to give you a general overview of the many dimensions of woodworking and basics you need to know to operate as a woodworker.

First, you need to understand the fundamental element of woodworking, the wood itself. In chapter one, you will find wood species divided into hardwoods and softwoods, domestic and foreign, with tips on which types of wood are best suited to your needs and your projects.

From there, you'll find the nitty-gritty and not-always-fun aspects of woodworking — topics like fasteners and glues, as well as, ugh, shop math. But if you're going to create those wood works of art, you'll have to put a little science, and a little math, into it. The end result is always worth it.

This book will also explore the more aesthetic aspects of woodworking, such as the creativity of designing your own piece of furniture.

In addition to a detailed resource and source listing, you'll also find definitions and descriptions of the multitude of joints that you can create to hold your furniture together, as well as hand tool, power tool, sharpening, finishing and shop safety information.

Throughout this book, the dry details of what you need to work wood will be interspersed with interesting stories about furniture styles and movements, furniture history, famed furniture designers and more.

❯ THE BASICS OF **woodworking**

Why do woodworkers work wood? It seems like a simple question, but it doesn't have a simple answer.

Woodworking means something different to everyone who does it, and to everyone who admires it.

Particularly to today's woodworker, it's not so much about creating utilitarian objects of necessity as it is about the act of creating itself. The process of woodworking seems to be very important to today's woodworker, not just the end product.

According to a 1940s Deltagram, woodworking prevented many stir-crazy men not able to fight during World War II from committing suicide. That may be an extreme example, but it points out that the need for more furniture wasn't the driving force.

But, initially, we can assume that woodworking began as a way to fill a civilized need.

From the relatively crude, and purely utilitarian, wooden creations of the early Middle Ages, furniture making and woodworking in general evolved into the highly ornate furniture seen during the Renaissance and through to the present day.

It's interesting to note that the techniques used to join pieces of wood together to create furniture and other useful objects evolved notably between the 12th and 15th centuries.

And, now, in the 21st century, the techniques and tools available to woodworkers seem almost infinite. But to take advantage of everything that's out there, without breaking the bank, you need to know what's available and what you plan to build, and deduce from there what's necessary for your shop and what's not.

While collecting tools is entertainment in itself, a little frugality and common sense can help you make smart decisions when adding to your woodworking arsenal.

If you're new to woodworking, you don't need to buy every tool that exists. Start with the basics, tools that can contribute to almost any project: screwdrivers, measuring devices and a combination square, a workbench of some sort, clamps, an open space within which to build, a circular saw, a jigsaw, a drill and accompanying bits, safety glasses (of course), a file, a mallet, a bevel gauge, some hand planes, chisels and sandpaper (or, if you want to get a little less exercise, an orbital sander). A table saw is a great thing to have, but you can survive without it.

Whether you're new to the craft or an old hand, it can be a good idea to look up your local woodworking club or guild and go to a few meetings. Members share ideas, help solve problems and often have useful guest speakers or offer seminars in headache-inducing dilemmas, such as incorporating the proper finishing techniques into a particular project.

Ask around for a local club, check your yellow pages under "wood," or try a quick search on the Internet. One Web site that has a good listing of woodworking clubs organized by state is www.woodturns.com.

Another great idea is to take a woodworking class at your local community education outlet or community college. You'll learn some basics, some tricks and probably meet a few cool woodworking buddies.

CHAPTER 1

> wood
species, uses and characteristics

For most woodworkers, this is what it's all about ... the texture, the smell, the simple working of the wood itself. But you can't just get lost in the romance of handling this medium; a lot of science is involved in why certain types of woods work better than others for different projects, and why certain types of woods are easier to work with than others.

This chapter will explain the fundamentals of the species, characteristics and properties of the most common hardwoods, softwoods and imports, as well as provide a brief overview of plywood.

types of wood available

More than 100 wood species are available in the United States, with about 60 native woods sold commercially. That's a lot of wood for woodworkers to choose from, and the right choice for a project might not always be the wood that first catches your eye.

Trees, and the wood they provide, are generally divided into two very broad, and sometimes confusing, classes: hardwoods and softwoods. The nomenclature is a result of the way in which the tree grows, as you will see.

The confusion comes from the fact that there are several softwoods that are actually "harder" than some hardwoods.

The heartwood of a tree is the older and inactive (because the cells are dead) central wood of the tree. The sapwood of a tree is the wood surrounding the heartwood. In the living tree, the sapwood carries the sap between the roots and the crown. It is usually lighter in color (often creamy or off-white) than the heartwood.

HARDWOODS

Hardwoods are deciduous trees with broad leaves. Hardwoods, which are angiosperms with seeds enclosed in the ovary of the flower, produce a fruit or a nut and usually go dormant (lose their leaves) in the winter. Hardwoods are also porous, meaning they contain wood cells with open ends called vessel elements that serve as conduits for transporting water or sap in the tree.

Some examples of hardwoods are oak, ash, cherry, maple and poplar. Most imported tropical woods are hardwoods.

U.S. hardwoods are generally used for woodworking: for furniture making, cabinetmaking, built-in projects, paneling and architectural woodwork.

Imported woods, sometimes dramatically referred to as "exotic" woods, are mostly hardwoods.

SOFTWOODS

Softwoods, on the other hand, are generally evergreen conifers, meaning they are cone-bearing. Softwoods are nonporous, meaning they do not contain the vessel elements found in hardwoods.

Softwoods are generally used in the construction of flooring and moulding, but also in paneling and cabinetry work. The most common U.S. softwoods available include cedar, fir, hemlock, pine, redwood and spruce.

PLYWOOD

Plywood, which can be made from either hardwoods or softwoods, is basically any flat panel layered with sheets of veneer (called "plies"), joined by pressure and some sort of adhesive.

Layers are constructed with the direction of the grain opposite (perpendicular to) one another. The Forest Products Laboratory in Madison, Wisconsin, points out an interesting fact: Plywood is always constructed with an odd number of layers, but since layers can consist of a single ply or of two or more plies laminated such that their grain is parallel, a panel can contain an odd or even number of plies.

Most plywood manufactured for industrial or construction use is produced domestically and is usually made from softwoods such as fir, southern pine and redwood, although hardwoods can also be used. Hardwood plywood is made from several different species and is usually intended for decorative uses, such as furniture, cabinet panels and wall panels.

Plywood's main advantages over solid wood are its high strength-to-weight and strength-to-thickness ratios.

WHERE DO HARDWOODS GROW?

Hardwood forests cover more than 269 million acres of the United States. Most U.S. hardwoods grow in states along and east of the Mississippi River. Alder, which grows principally in the Pacific Northwest, is the only major commercial hardwood species that grows in the western U.S.

Each species requires different soil, climate and sunlight conditions to thrive. This is why you won't see willow in the hardwood forests of the Great Lakes States, and why hard maple doesn't grow in the Mississippi Delta.

Trees are the earth's oxygen factory. To grow a pound of wood, a tree uses 1.47 pounds of carbon dioxide and gives off 1.07 pounds of oxygen. A pound of oxygen is what one person breathes in a day. An acre of trees can remove 13 tons of dust and gases from the atmosphere each year. Through shading and water transpiration, forests cool the environment. The leaves of a 100' tree have the same cooling effect as an average home's central air conditioner.

In addition, forests are nature's water filter. The forest floor absorbs up to 18" of precipitation before gradually releasing it into natural channels and water courses. In the growing season, an acre of beech or maple trees can give off 8,000 gallons of water through transpiration.

Responsible forestry ensures that one of our most renewable resources will indeed be plentiful for generations to come.

Courtesy of the Hardwood Manufacturers Association, www.hardwoodinfo.com.

lumber measurements

SOFTWOOD LUMBER

When purchasing softwood lumber, know that "nominal sizes" were originally derived from rough lumber dimensions *before* surfacing took place, and so these size listings are always a greater number than the actual dimensions of the lumber. For example, you may think you're buying a 2×4, but a dry 2" × 4" is actually surfaced to a final measurement of $1\frac{1}{2}$" × $3\frac{1}{2}$".

SURFACED LUMBER

Surfaced lumber has been surfaced by a machine, of course, for smoothness and uniformity. If it's referred to as S1S, you're getting a board that is surfaced on one side only. If it's referred to as S2S, you're getting a board that has been surfaced on both sides. If it's referred to as S1E, you're getting a board that has one edge surfaced, and S2E means two edges have been surfaced. A combination of sides and edges would be referred to as one of the following: S1S1E, S1S2E, S2S1E or S4S.

BOARDS

What you buy at the lumberyard or wood store is referred to as a board if the lumber is $1\frac{1}{2}$" or less in its actual thickness, and greater than $1\frac{1}{2}$" in its width. If the piece of lumber is less than $5\frac{1}{2}$" in width, then it may be referred to as a strip rather than a board.

ROUGH LUMBER

Rough lumber has not been surfaced, but it has been sawed and edged, often showing saw marks.

BOARD FOOT

A board foot is the inch-pound volume measurement for hardwoods. A board foot is the equivalent of a board that is one foot long, one foot wide and one inch thick. This equals, in volume, 144 cubic inches of wood.

STANDARD LUMBER LENGTHS

Note that fractional lengths are always rounded down, not up. Standard lengths are in feet: 4, 5, 6, 7, 8, 9, 10, 11, 12, 13, 14, 15 and 16.

STANDARD THICKNESS VALUES FOR ROUGH AND SURFACED HARDWOOD

ROUGH LUMBER		SURFACED LUMBER	
(MM)	(INCHES)	(MM)	(INCHES)
9.5	$\frac{3}{8}$	4.8	$\frac{3}{16}$
12.7	$\frac{1}{2}$	7.9	$\frac{5}{16}$
15.9	$\frac{5}{8}$	11.1	$\frac{7}{16}$
19.0	$\frac{3}{4}$	14.3	$\frac{9}{16}$
25.4	1	20.6	$\frac{13}{16}$
31.8	$1\frac{1}{4}$	27.0	$1\frac{1}{16}$
38.1	$1\frac{1}{2}$	33.3	$1\frac{5}{16}$
44.4	$1\frac{3}{4}$	38.1	$1\frac{1}{2}$
50.8	2	44.4	$1\frac{3}{4}$
63.5	$2\frac{1}{2}$	57.2	$2\frac{1}{4}$
76.2	3	69.8	$2\frac{3}{4}$
88.9	$3\frac{1}{2}$	82.6	$3\frac{1}{4}$
101.6	4	95.2	$3\frac{3}{4}$

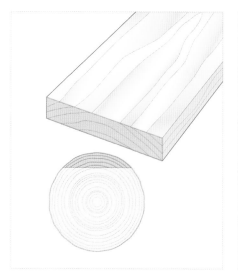

Flat-sawn or plain-sawn lumber offers the most common grain pattern, which gives a surface oriented tangent to the tree's rings, as shown above.

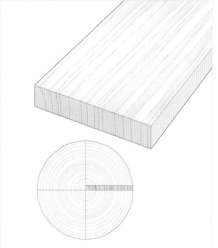

Quarter-sawn lumber is run through the mill so that the surface is perpendicular to the tree's rings, as shown above. This gives an appealing, consistent grain pattern.

Rift-sawn lumber gives a grain pattern that is similar on all four sides of the piece of lumber, with a linear grain pattern.

hardwoods

RED ALDER

Alnus rubra

COLOR: from off-white to pale-pink brownish color

GROWS: on the Pacific coast from Alaska to California

PROPERTIES: moderately lightweight; of medium strength; low shock resistance

USES: mostly furniture, also for millwork

WHITE ASH

Fraxinus americana

COLOR: heartwood is brown; sapwood is off-white

GROWS: in eastern U.S.

PROPERTIES: heavy; stiff; strong; shock resistant

USES: mostly for oars, sporting implements such as baseball bats, decorative veneer, furniture and cabinetry

ASPEN

Populus grandidentata

COLOR: heartwood is off-gray/brown; sapwood is lighter in color

GROWS: in the Northeast

PROPERTIES: uniform texture; easy to work; lightweight

USES: mostly furniture, also for millwork, particleboard and veneer

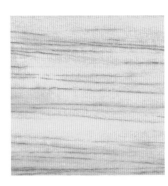

BALSA WOOD

Ochroma lagopus

COLOR: pale beige to pink

GROWS: South and Central America

PROPERTIES: the lightest commercial hardwood

USES: insulation, model-making, packaging

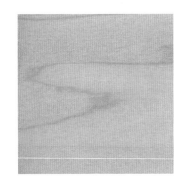

BASSWOOD

Tilia americana

COLOR: heartwood is yellow-brown with dark streaks; sapwood is white or brown

GROWS: eastern U.S., from Canada south

PROPERTIES: soft; lightweight; straight-grained and easy to work

USES: moulding and woodenware, including woodcarving and veneers

BEECH

Fagus grandifolia

COLOR: heartwood is reddish brown; sapwood is white

GROWS: eastern U.S.

PROPERTIES: heavy; hard and strong; good for steam-bending and wood-turning

USES: for flooring, veneer, containers and furniture making

YELLOW BIRCH

Betula alleghaniensis

COLOR: heartwood is reddish brown; sapwood is white

GROWS: in the Northeast and Great Lakes States, and Appalachian Mountains

PROPERTIES: heavy, hard and strong with uniform texture

USES: furniture, boxes, doors and other interior woodwork, and veneer

BUTTERNUT

Juglans cinerea

COLOR: heartwood is light brown; sapwood is off-white

GROWS: from Canada to Maine, west to Minnesota

PROPERTIES: lightweight; coarse in texture; machines and finishes easily

USES: furniture, cabinets, veneer and interior woodwork

Did you know?

As you'll notice in this chapter, the heartwood of a species is often where the real color is, whereas the sapwood is often less striking, although consistent, in its commonly off-white color.

CHERRY

Prunus serotina

COLOR: heartwood is reddish brown; sapwood is white

GROWS: southeastern Canada, eastern U.S.

PROPERTIES: strong and stiff; uniform in texture; machines well

USES: furniture, veneer, caskets, architectural woodwork

CHESTNUT

Castanea dentata

COLOR: heartwood is gray-brown; sapwood is off-white

GROWS: previously in east U.S.; 1920s blight killed almost all; today, comes mostly from salvaged timbers

PROPERTIES: lightweight, little strength, easy to work

USES: furniture, caskets and veneer core stock; mostly interior woodwork

ELM

Ulmus americana

COLOR: heartwood is light brown with red; sapwood is off-white

GROWS: in eastern U.S.

PROPERTIES: moderately hard, stiff and heavy; good for bending

USES: mostly veneer for furniture and decorative panels

HICKORY

Carya ovata

COLOR: heartwood is red; sapwood is white

GROWS: eastern, central and southern U.S.

PROPERTIES: heavy; hard and strong

USES: mostly for tool handles, dowels and some furniture; also for flavoring meat

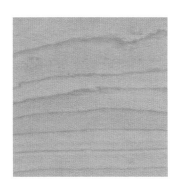

HARD MAPLE

Acer saccharum

COLOR: heartwood is light reddish brown; sapwood is white with reddish tinge

GROWS: in eastern U.S. and Great Lakes States

PROPERTIES: heavy; strong, stiff and shock resistant; grain is straight, but bird's-eye, curly and fiddleback maple have decorative qualities woodworkers love for furniture making and other wood projects

USES: lumber, veneer, furniture, cabinets, cutting boards, bowling alleys and bobbins

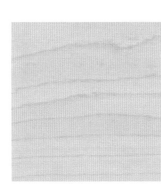

SOFT MAPLE

Acer saccharinum

COLOR: heartwood is light reddish brown (lighter than hard maple); sapwood is white with reddish tinge

GROWS: in eastern U.S.

PROPERTIES: similar to hard maple, but not as heavy, hard or strong

USES: veneer, some furniture, railroad cross ties

> HARDWOODS CONTINUED

RED OAK

Quercus rubra

COLOR: heartwood is reddish brown; sapwood is off-white

GROWS: in eastern U.S.

PROPERTIES: heavy; quarter-sawn lumber evident by broad rays in grain

USES: lumber, veneer, millwork, furniture and caskets

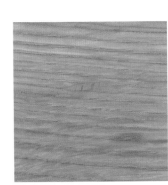

WHITE OAK

Quercus alba

COLOR: heartwood is gray-brown; sapwood is white

GROWS: in the South Atlantic and central states

PROPERTIES: heavy and very impermeable to liquids

USES: cooperage, veneer, shipbuilding, furniture and millwork

PECAN

Carya illinoensis

COLOR: heartwood is reddish brown with dark brown stripes; sapwood is white or creamy white with pinkish tones

GROWS: southern U.S.

PROPERTIES: open grain; occasionally wavy or irregular

USES: chairs and bentwood furniture

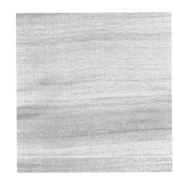

YELLOW POPLAR

Liriodendron tulipifera

COLOR: heartwood is yellow-brown; sapwood is white

GROWS: in east, south and midwestern U.S.

PROPERTIES: straight-grained; uniform in texture

USES: mostly for furniture, moulding, cabinets and musical instruments; also used for plywood

SASSAFRAS

Sassafras albidum

COLOR: heartwood is dull brown; sapwood is light yellow

GROWS: in eastern U.S., and from southeastern Iowa to eastern Texas

PROPERTIES: moderately hard and heavy; resistant to decay

USES: small boats, fence posts and millwork

SWEETGUM

Liquidambar styraciflua

COLOR: heartwood is reddish brown; sapwood is light colored

GROWS: from Connecticut to Missouri and south to the Gulf Coast

PROPERTIES: moderately heavy and hard

USES: quarter-sawn pieces are great for furniture and woodwork, also used for veneer and plywood

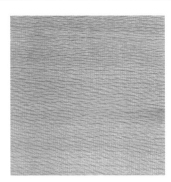

SYCAMORE

Platanus occidentalis

COLOR: heartwood is reddish brown; sapwood is lighter colored

GROWS: from Maine to Nebraska, south to Florida and Texas

PROPERTIES: interlocked grain and nice texture; moderately hard and heavy

USES: lumber, veneer, fuel and furniture; also small boxes and butcher blocks

BLACK WALNUT

Juglans nigra

COLOR: heartwood is light to dark brown; sapwood is off-white

GROWS: from Vermont south and to the Great Plains

PROPERTIES: straight-grained and easy to work; heavy; hard and stiff; good for natural finishing

USES: valued for furniture and architectural woodwork because of its interesting grain patterns; also used for gun stocks and interior woodwork

TUPELO

Nyssa aquatica

COLOR: heartwood is light brown; sapwood is lighter colored

GROWS: in the southeastern U.S.

PROPERTIES: interlocked grain; uniform in texture; moderately heavy and strong

USES: lumber, veneer, furniture, pallets and crates

WILLOW

Salix alba

COLOR: heartwood is gray-brown; sapwood is creamy yellow

GROWS: in the Mississippi Valley

PROPERTIES: uniform in texture; slightly interlocked grain; lightweight

USES: lumber and veneer, as well as furniture, boxes and caskets

softwoods

EASTERN RED CEDAR

Juniperus virginiana

COLOR: heartwood is red; sapwood is off-white

GROWS: in eastern U.S.

PROPERTIES: moderately heavy and strong; uniform in texture; often has many small knots; resistant to decay

USES: mostly fence posts, but also chests, wardrobes and small wood projects like pencils

WESTERN RED CEDAR

Thuja plicata

COLOR: heartwood is reddish brown; sapwood is off-white

GROWS: from the Pacific Coast to Alaska

PROPERTIES: straight-grained; uniform in texture; lightweight; resistant to decay

USES: interior woodwork; shipbuilding; doors

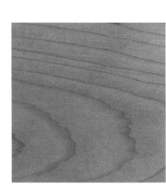

WHITE CEDAR

Thuja occidentalis

COLOR: heartwood is light brown; sapwood is mostly white

GROWS: from Maine south along the Appalachians and west to the Great Lakes States

PROPERTIES: lightweight; low in strength; works easily

USES: cabin logs, woodenware, boats, fencing

CYPRESS

Taxodium distichum

COLOR: heartwood varies from yellow to dark brown; sapwood is mostly white

GROWS: in the southern U.S.

PROPERTIES: moderately hard, heavy and strong

USES: siding, millwork and interior woodwork

DOUGLAS FIR

Pseudotsuga menziesii

COLOR: heartwood is reddish or yellow; sapwood is lighter in color

GROWS: from Mexico to the Pacific Coast

PROPERTIES: varies widely

USES: lumber, plywood, general millwork, and sometimes in furniture

HEMLOCK

Tsuga heterophylla

COLOR: heartwood and sapwood are both white, with a reddish-purple coloring

GROWS: along Pacific Coast and in Rocky Mountains

PROPERTIES: lightweight and moderately strong and hard

USES: plywood and lumber for furniture, boxes and ladders

LARCH

Larix occidentalis

COLOR: heartwood is light brown; sapwood is a dirty white

GROWS: Idaho, Montana, Oregon and Washington

PROPERTIES: moderately strong; hard and heavy; splits easily; straight-grained

USES: building construction, interior woodwork, flooring and doors

PONDEROSA PINE

Pinus ponderosa

COLOR: heartwood is light red and brown; sapwood is mostly white

GROWS: in the western U.S.

PROPERTIES: moderately lightweight and soft; uniform in texture; straight-grained

USES: lumber and veneer; some interior woodwork

REDWOOD

Sequoia sempervirens

COLOR: heartwood is light red to deep brown; sapwood is mostly white

GROWS: on the coast of California

PROPERTIES: straight-grained; easy to work; fairly decay resistant

USES: mostly construction and outdoor furniture

SUGAR PINE

Pinus lambertiana

COLOR: heartwood is light brown; sapwood is white

GROWS: in California and Oregon

PROPERTIES: uniform in texture; straight-grained; easy to work; good for nailing

USES: general millwork, boxes, doors and frames

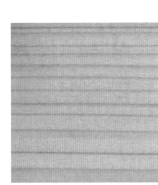

SITKA SPRUCE

Picea sitchensis

COLOR: heartwood is light brown; sapwood is white

GROWS: along northwest coast from California to Alaska

PROPERTIES: moderately lightweight and soft; uniform in texture

USES: mostly lumber, pulpwood, furniture, millwork and aircraft construction

WHITE PINE

Pinus strobus

COLOR: heartwood is off-white to reddish; sapwood is off-white

GROWS: mostly in Idaho and Washington

PROPERTIES: straight-grained and easy to work

USES: lumber, millwork, interior woodwork

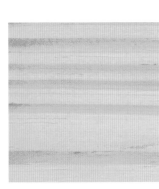

SOUTHERN PINE

FOUR MAJOR SPECIES

(Pinus palustris, longleaf; Pinus echinata, shortleaf; Pinus taeda, loblolly; and Pinus elliottii, slash pine)

COLOR: heartwood is reddish brown; sapwood is off-white

GROWS: throughout eastern and southern U.S.

PROPERTIES: longleaf and slash are heavy, strong and hard; shortleaf and loblolly are more lightweight

USES: structural-grade plywood, extensive range of construction uses, interior woodwork, boxes and pallets

imports

BUBINGA
Guibourtia

COLOR: ranges from light red to brown with purple streaks

GROWS: in west Africa

PROPERTIES: moderately hard and heavy, but fairly easy to work

USES: furniture, veneers and turning

PADAUK
Pterocarpus soyauxii

COLOR: deep red-brown

GROWS: in Africa

PROPERTIES: coarse in texture with interlocking grain; easy to work; finishes well

USES: veneer, fine cabinetry and other woodwork

JELUTONG
Dyera costulata

COLOR: whitish

GROWS: in Malaysia

PROPERTIES: straight-grained; moderately uniform in texture

USES: making patterns, wooden shoes and picture frames

PURPLEHEART
Peltogyne

COLOR: brown when first cut, then turns a deep purple, then a dark brown over time

GROWS: from Mexico to Brazil

PROPERTIES: moderately difficult to work; good for turning; takes finishes well

USES: turning, marquetry, fine furniture, some shipbuilding

HONDURAN MAHOGANY
Swietenia macrophylla

COLOR: light pink to dark reddish brown

GROWS: Mexico, Central America and South America

PROPERTIES: fine to coarse texture; decay resistant; very easy to work; takes finish well

USES: fine furniture, musical instruments, veneers, turning and carving

BRAZILIAN ROSEWOOD
Dalbergia nigra

COLOR: heartwood is brown or purple with black streaks; sapwood is white

GROWS: in Brazil

PROPERTIES: coarse; straight-grained; oily; hard; heavy and strong

USES: mostly plywood veneer, turning

LUAN MAHOGANY
Shorea

COLOR: extremely varied

GROWS: in Southeast Asia

PROPERTIES: part of the meranti group of wood; interlocked grain

USES: furniture, cabinetry, moulding and some decking

INDIAN ROSEWOOD
Dalbergia latifolia

COLOR: heartwood is brown to purple with dark streaks; sapwood is yellowish

GROWS: in India

PROPERTIES: heavy and strong; moderately difficult to work; good for turning

USES: mostly veneer

TEAK

Tectona grandis

COLOR: yellow to dark brown

GROWS: India, Myanmar, Thailand, Laos, Cambodia, Vietnam and the East Indies

PROPERTIES: coarse texture; straight-grained; oily; moderately easy to work

USES: shipbuilding, furniture and decorative veneer

WENGE

Milletia laurentii

COLOR: deep brown with black striping

GROWS: in Africa

PROPERTIES: hard; coarse in texture; finishes well

USES: fine cabinetry, fine furniture, woodturning

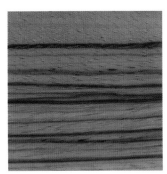

ZEBRAWOOD

Microberlinia brazzavillensis

COLOR: light brown with dark striping

GROWS: in Africa

PROPERTIES: hard; heavy and coarse in texture with interlocking grain; finishes well

USES: as inlay for decorative color contrast

WOODS OF THE WORLD

For detailed information about over 900 wood species, covering 95 percent of all the wood in trade, order the Woods of the World CD on-line at www.forestworld.com. This is the most comprehensive place to learn about wood names, common uses and woodworking properties and to see full-color pictures and more than 3,000 pages of text. Search the CD's database by a variety of properties, including up to 10,000 common names. There are two versions for purchase; one is $49.95 and the other is $29.95 (with fewer species and less information). If you aren't on-line, call ForestWorld at 802-382-8888.

plywood

Plywood, put simply, is a structural material made of sheets of wood glued or cemented together with the grains of adjacent layers arranged at right angles to one another.

Plywood is always made of an odd number of layers, and each layer consists of one or more sheets of veneer. A veneer is just a thin sheet of wood.

Layers are glued together with the grain of adjacent layers placed at right angles (or, perpendicular). The reason for this alternation of grain direction is strength and stability, which means less chance of splitting. The outside plies are called face or back plies and the inner plies are called cores or centers. Cores may be made of veneer, lumber or particleboard. Total panel thicknesses are usually at least $1/16$" thick and not more than 3" thick.

TYPES OF PLYWOOD

There are two broad categories of plywood: construction/industrial plywood and hardwood/decorative plywood. Most woodworkers are interested in the latter. Hardwood plywood is made from a variety of wood species, both domestic and foreign.

ROTARY PEELING

The veneer that is used for plywood, for efficiency reasons, is usually rotary peeled, not sliced or sawn.

Logs chosen as peeler logs are first cut into $8^1/2$' blocks. These blocks are then placed in a huge, industrial-strength lathe, which rotates the block against a long cutter knife that peels the log like a cucumber. The veneer (in this state, the wood is now referred to as "veneer") is peeled off in continuous sheets at a speed of anywhere up to 13 linear feet per second.

Softwood veneer may range in thickness from $1/16$" to $3/16$", and hardwood veneer is often even thinner than that. Then the veneer is transported to clippers that cut it into a variety of widths.

The veneer is dried from 2 percent to 5 percent moisture content, then graded according to quality (see Veneer Grades, at right). Adhesive is applied to the veneer, and then plywood panels are manufactured.

PLYWOOD TYPES

A-A: This is a sanded plywood with face and back plies that are A-Grade and inner plies that are D-Grade. Bonded with either exterior or interior glue. Used for cabinets and furniture.

A-A Exterior: This is a sanded plywood with face and back plies that are A-Grade and inner plies that are C-Grade. Bonded with exterior glue. Used for cabinets, containers, boats and fences.

A-B: This is a sanded plywood with a face that is A-Grade, a back that is B-Grade and inner plies that are D-Grade. Bonded with interior or exterior glue.

A-B Exterior: This is a sanded plywood with a face that is A-Grade, a back that is B-Grade and inner plies that are C-Grade.

VENEER GRADES

A-GRADE VENEER: This is the highest-quality veneer. Basically, it has no knots or similar imperfections. It is intended to be used as a paintable surface.

N-GRADE VENEER: This is also the highest-quality veneer, but it is intended to be used as a natural finish surface.

B-GRADE VENEER: This is a solid surface, obviously a grade below A and N, meaning it allows for small, round knots, patches and round plugs.

C-PLUGGED-GRADE VENEER: This is an improved C-grade veneer.

C-GRADE VENEER: This midquality veneer is the lowest-quality veneer allowed in the construction of exterior-type plywood. It allows for small knots, knotholes and patches.

D-GRADE VENEER: This is the lowest-quality veneer. It cannot be used in the construction of exterior-type plywood. It has larger knots and knotholes.

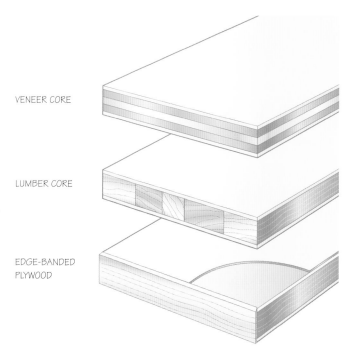

VENEER CORE

LUMBER CORE

EDGE-BANDED PLYWOOD

Veneer core plywood is layers of wood veneer sandwiched together with the top and bottom veneers being the best. The lumber core is made of edge-glued boards sandwiched between top and bottom layers of top-quality hardwood veneers. Hardwood edge-banding can be applied after the plywood parts have been cut to size. Another choice is to use iron-on veneer tape. It has heat-activated glue applied to the back of the veneer strips.

Bookmatched ve-
neers are opened
like the pages of a
book, so that they
appear to reflect
each other. This is an
attractive pattern
that is considered a
classic use of ve-
neers. When veneers
are bookmatched,
the grain is reversed
on every other piece

of veneer. When finish is applied, the light is diffused in
opposite directions and the veneers don't appear to
be the same colors. This is something to consider
when choosing your veneers.

Slipmatching veneer
is exactly what it says
— each piece of ve-
neer is slipped off
and placed next to
the preceding piece
of veneer with the
same face out and
the grain running
the same direction.
This method gives
the veneer pieces a
consistent color, but

the lines between the pieces of veneer are more
prominent. Large wall panels are commonly done in
this manner.

Bonded with exterior glue.

A-C Exterior: This is a sanded plywood with a face that is A-Grade and a
back and inner plies that are C-Grade.
Bonded with exterior glue. Used for high-
moisture situations.

B-B: This is a sanded plywood with a
face and back that are B-Grade and inner
plies that are D-Grade. Bonded with interior or exterior glue.

B-B Exterior: This is a sanded plywood
with a face and back that are B-Grade and
inner plies that are C-Grade. Bonded with
exterior glue.

B-C Exterior: This is plywood with a
sanded face that is B-Grade and a back and

inner plies that are C-Grade. Bonded with
exterior glue.

B-D: This is plywood with a sanded
face that is B-Grade and a back and inner
plies that are D-Grade. Bonded with interior or exterior glue.

C-C Plugged Exterior: This is a touch-
sanded plywood with a face that is C-
Plugged-Grade and with back and inner
plies that are C-Grade. Bonded with exteri-
or glue. Used for high-moisture situations.

C-D Plugged: This is a touch-sanded
plywood with a face that is C-Plugged-
Grade and a back and inner plies that
are D-Grade. Bonded with interior or
exterior glue.

APA GUIDES ENGINEERED WOOD PRODUCTS

For nearly 70 years, APA–The Engineered Wood
Association, has focused on helping the industry
create structural wood products of exceptional
strength, versatility and reliability. Combining
the research efforts of scientists at APA's 37,000-
square-foot research center with the knowledge
gained from decades of fieldwork and cooperation with member manufacturers, APA promotes
new solutions and improved processes.

The APA and APA Engineered Wood Systems
(EWS) trademarks show that products that bear
them have met specific manufacturing and product performance guidelines carefully delineated
in specification guides available to architects,
builders and engineers. Only products manufactured by APA and APA EWS members committed
to APA's rigorous program of quality inspection
and testing may bear the respective trademarks
of quality and performance assurance.

APA members are comprised of well-known
industry leaders, whose mills produce approximately 75 percent of the structural wood panel
products manufactured in North America, plus
a host of new products that include glued laminated timber (glulam), composite panels, wood
I-joists, and laminated veneer lumber. APA also
works in close cooperation with its related corporation, EWS. EWS members produce more
than 70 percent of the glulam and the majority
of the wood I-joists manufactured in North
America.

With over 400 publications, extensive
research and technical reports, comprehensive
market studies and more, APA has the information you need about engineered wood products.

Visit www.apawood.org for more information.

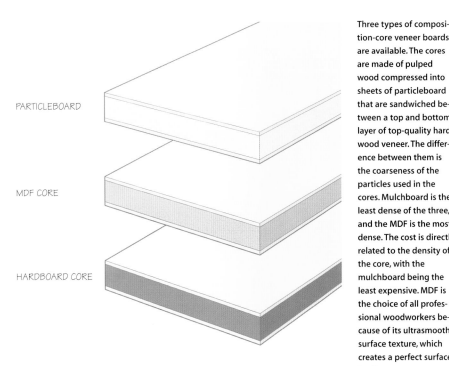

PARTICLEBOARD

MDF CORE

HARDBOARD CORE

Three types of composi-
tion-core veneer boards
are available. The cores
are made of pulped
wood compressed into
sheets of particleboard
that are sandwiched be-
tween a top and bottom
layer of top-quality hardwood veneer. The differ-
ence between them is
the coarseness of the
particles used in the
cores. Mulchboard is the
least dense of the three,
and the MDF is the most
dense. The cost is directly
related to the density of
the core, with the
mulchboard being the
least expensive. MDF is
the choice of all profes-
sional woodworkers be-
cause of its ultrasmooth
surface texture, which
creates a perfect surface
for fine veneers.

Glulam radial arches span this two-lane highway
bridge in Colorado.

⊙ THE FURNITURE CITY: GRAND RAPIDS

This is an exterior view of the Van Andel Museum Center, on the Grand River in downtown Grand Rapids, Michigan.

IMAGE COURTESY OF PUBLIC MUSEUM OF GRAND RAPIDS

The first center of furniture manufacturing in North America was in Grand Rapids, Michigan. Grand Rapids led the nation in furniture production from 1870 to 1935, and has long been known as the Furniture City.

The Van Andel Museum Center is the principal facility of the Public Museum of Grand Rapids, which was founded in 1854. The Van Andel Museum Center opened in 1994 and is a state-of-the-art facility.

Occupying the single largest space in the museum, *The Furniture City* is a permanent exhibit that tells the story of how furniture manufacturing affected the people of Grand Rapids and shaped the growth of the community from 1840 to the present.

Highlights of the exhibition include the following:

• A 30-foot, 35-ton Corliss-type steam engine with an 18-foot flywheel, which serves as the exhibition's symbolic heart.

• The re-created Phoenix factory interior, which includes an elaborate overhead system of pulleys and line shafts, which convey power from the steam engine, over a visitor passageway to functioning woodworking machinery from the 19th and early 20th centuries.

• On-site periodical demonstrations of furniture making, from machine cutting to hand decorating, by local machinists and retired furniture workers.

• More than 120 examples selected from the Public Museum's extensive Grand Rapids–made furniture collection, ranging from the 1840s to the 1990s.

• A 31' by 16' painted mural telling the allegorical story of the Furniture City, commissioned by the museum and painted by local artist Ed Wong-Ligda of Grand Valley State University.

• Multimedia presentations and hands-on games and activities for children and adults, including a completely detailed miniature factory.

• References to classical architecture of downtown Grand Rapids buildings during the era of the Grand Rapids Furniture Market.

• Vignette re-creating a 1920s showroom from the Grand Rapids Furniture Market.

• Painted silk banners from furniture industry labor unions.

• Systems Furniture Workstations do-

nated by local industry leaders.

• Periodically changing display on the future of the Grand Rapids furniture industry.

In 1998, the Public Museum of Grand Rapids published *Grand Rapids Furniture: The Story of America's Furniture City*, a major historical reference work.

Funding for *The Furniture City* exhibit was provided by the National Endowment for the Humanities, the U.S. Department of Energy, the State of Michigan Equity Program, NBD Bank, N.A. and the Grand Rapids Furniture Manufacturers Association.

For more information, contact the Museum Center at 616-456-3977 or visit www.grmuseum.org.

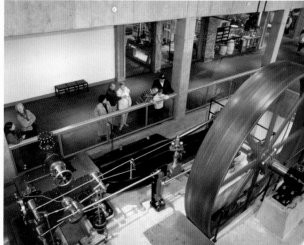

A 30', 35-ton 1905 Corliss-type steam engine with an 18' flywheel serves as the exhibit's symbolic heart, appearing to provide power to the partially operational re-creation of the Phoenix Furniture Factory circa 1910.

IMAGE COURTESY OF PUBLIC MUSEUM OF GRAND RAPIDS

GRAND RAPIDS FURNITURE COMPANIES

▪ **BAKER FURNITURE, INC.** Begun in 1890 as Cook, Baker & Co. of Allegan, Michigan, Baker moved its factories to Holland, Michigan in 1933. Today Baker Furniture, Inc. continues to operate as a subsidiary of Kohler Co., with headquarters in Grand Rapids and factories in Holland. Although Baker has manufactured some significant modern lines of residential furniture, it has been best known since the 1920s for its reproductions of 18th-century American and European antiques.

▪ **BERKEY & GAY FURNITURE CO.** Operating as a partnership between Julius Berkey and Alphonso Hamm in 1861, it took the name of Berkey & Gay in 1866. It soon became one of the largest manufacturers of residential furniture in the country, making primarily bedroom and dining room suites in Renaissance Revival and other Victorian Revival styles. It added upholstering divisions in the early 20th century, and continued as a leading producer of Colonial and European Revival home furniture until declaring bankruptcy in 1931. Revived in 1934, it never achieved its former glory, closing its doors for good in 1948.

▪ **CENTURY FURNITURE CO.** Founded in 1900 as a quality manufacturer of residential furniture in a wide range of European Revival styles. Century furniture was well built, with expensive materials and lavish decoration. It declared bankruptcy in 1942, and ceased production in 1945 when it was purchased by the Murray Furniture Co.

▪ **GRAND RAPIDS CHAIR CO.** The first products of the Grand Rapids Chair Co., founded in 1872, were caned chairs and upholstery frames for parlor suites. By the late 1880s, the company made a wide variety of upholstered and case pieces, but by the end of the 19th century, ads stated emphatically that the Grand Rapids Chair Co. no longer made chairs. In the early 20th century, it produced parlor, dining and living room suites in a variety of revival styles. Beginning in 1950, the company produced a line of modular residential units. A subsidiary of Sligh Furniture Co. from 1945 to 1957 and of Baker Furniture Co. from 1957, it became fully integrated into Baker in 1973.

▪ **IMPERIAL FURNITURE CO.** Founded in 1903, Imperial's large inventory of designs consisted primarily of dining and occasional tables, and associated case pieces such as bookcases and desks. Imperial also laid claim to the invention of the "coffee table" in the 1920s. Imperial was sold to Bergsma Brothers Co. of Grand Rapids in 1954, which operated its plant until 1983.

▪ **JOHNSON FURNITURE CO./JOHNSON-HANDLEY-JOHNSON** The three Swedish Johnson brothers began the Cabinetmakers Co. in Grand Rapids in 1903, changing its name to Johnson Furniture Co. in 1908. In that same year, English designer Tom Handley became the company's head of design, beginning a long period of production of English 18th-century styles. In 1922, the four men organized Johnson-Handley-Johnson as a companion company. In 1983, the company merged with Rose Manufacturing Co. to form RoseJohnson, Inc. which is now the La-Z-Boy Contract Group.

▪ **LIMBERT CO., CHARLES P.** Charles Limbert started his company in 1894 as a manufacturer of Mission and folk-design chairs. In 1902 the company introduced its Arts & Crafts line. The factory was moved from Grand Rapids to Holland, Michigan, in 1906, though its showrooms remained in Grand Rapids. Limbert's last Mission and Arts & Crafts designs were produced in 1918. After this time, the company made 17th- and 18th-century revival lines until it closed in 1944.

▪ **MICHIGAN CHAIR CO.** In 1890, the Grand Ledge Chair Co. of Grand Ledge, Michigan, moved to Grand Rapids and changed its name to Michigan Chair Co. In its first two decades, the company made chairs in a wide range of styles including Venetian, Medieval-folk, Mission, Prairie, Austrian Modern, Colonial, Empire and Golden Oak. Revivals of Adam, Windsor and Colonial styles were produced in the 1910s and 1920s, as well as an Art Deco line in the early 1930s. The company closed in 1938 and reopened in 1946, closing for good in 1972.

▪ **PHOENIX FURNITURE CO.** Started by William A. Berkey and from the assets of Atkins and Soule of Grand Rapids in 1872, Phoenix was successful filling a niche in early Grand Rapids production, producing upholstered parlor furniture. David Wolcott Kendall served as chief designer from 1879 until his death in 1910, positioning the company as an innovator in Oriental-influenced Reform and Mission furniture. The company became a part of the Robert W. Irwin Furniture Co. in 1919, which continued to operate its factory until 1953.

▪ **SLIGH FURNITURE CO.** Sligh began in Grand Rapids as a manufacturer of inexpensive bedroom case furniture and bedroom suites. By the mid-1920s, Sligh claimed to be the largest manufacturer of furniture exclusively for the bedroom in the world. The company closed due to the Depression in 1932, then reopened as the Charles R. Sligh Co. in Holland,

The chair above is an example of the furniture that made Grand Rapids famous.

IMAGE COURTESY OF PUBLIC MUSEUM OF GRAND RAPIDS

Michigan, in 1933. Today Sligh Furniture and its Sligh Clock Division continue to operate in Holland and Zeeland, Michigan, making wooden office furniture and grandfather clocks.

▪ **STICKLEY BROTHERS FURNITURE CO.** Albert and John George Stickley, two of the five Stickley brothers who made furniture in the U.S., opened the Stickley Brothers Furniture Co. in Grand Rapids in 1891 to produce occasional chairs and fancy tables in Colonial and Mission styles. The company began its trademark "Quaint Mission" line in 1903, with residential furniture in oak sometimes augmented with hand-wrought copper hardware and Spanish leather upholstery. In 1914, the company began a line of revival pieces with Japanese painted decorations, as well as other revival styles, always under the "Quaint" trademark. Stickley ceased production in 1954.

▪ **WIDDICOMB FURNITURE CO.** George Widdicomb & Sons began cabinetmaking in 1857, closed during the Civil War and reopened as Widdicomb Brothers & Richards. In 1873, it incorporated as Widdicomb Furniture Co., a manufacturer of inexpensive bedroom furniture, making an assortment of Colonial and European revival styles. Lines designed in the 1940s and 1950s by T.H. Robsjohn Gibbings and George Nakashima made Widdicomb an important producer of Fifties-Modern furniture. The John Widdicomb Co. began in 1897 when brother John left Widdicomb to venture out on his own. The John Widdicomb Co. continues to operate in Grand Rapids today.

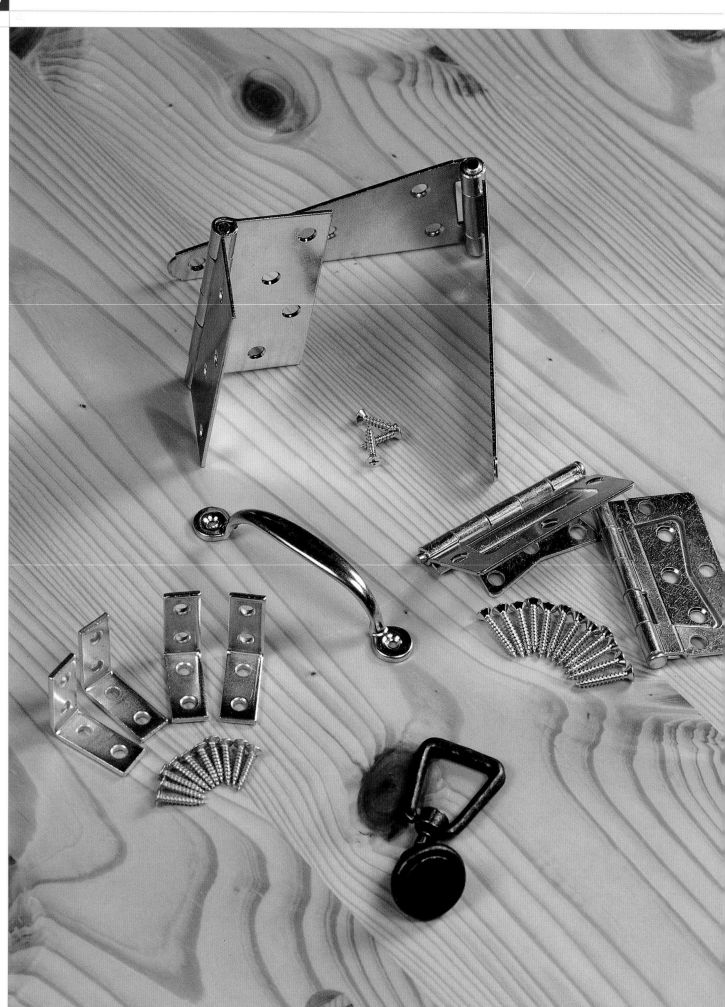

> hardware
fasteners, knobs and brackets

Hardware might not seem like the most glamorous aspect of a woodworking project, but in most cases it's an essential part of putting your final project together.

And if you put a little creativity and thought into your hardware choices, you might just add that final, classy flourish that brings your whole project together.

As Ann Rockler Jackson of Rockler Woodworking says, "I'm pretty fussy about the hardware that is used on a woodworking project. Some people might like nice jewelry; I like really good drawer slides!"

fasteners

NAILS

Nails are used mainly to join or fix pieces of wood together, usually softwoods, as hardwoods often cause the nails to bend under the hammer's impact and therefore aren't great for nailing.

Woodworkers concern themselves with basically four types of nails: common, casing, finishing and brads (which are tiny finish nails $\frac{1}{4}$" long or less).

Most common are, of course, the common nail and the finishing nail. Common nails have large, flat heads and are used for "unpretty" work that can look fairly rough. If a woodworker wants a prettier final project, the thinner finishing nails are a better choice (mainly because you can drive the small head deep into the wood and fill the gap with wood putty).

When shopping, note that nails are sold by head type and by penny weight.

SAVE YOUR PENNIES

Nails are sized on the penny system, which can be a little confusing unless you know this: A 2-penny nail (signified as "2d") is a nail that is 1" long. Any nail over 20d is called a spike.

Or you can try this little formula: For nail sizes that run up to 10-penny (signified as "10d"), you can figure out the nail's actual length by (1) dividing the penny size by 4 and (2) adding $\frac{1}{2}$" to that number. For example, a 4d nail would be $1\frac{1}{2}$" long.

And it works the other way, too. If you know the length of the nail you need and are trying to figure out which penny nail to buy at the hardware store, use the above formula in reverse: (1) subtract $\frac{1}{2}$" from the length of the nail and (2) multiply that number by 4. So, if you know you need a $2\frac{1}{2}$" nail, subtract that $\frac{1}{2}$" and multiply 2 by 4. Since 2 times 4 equals 8, you now know you need an 8d (8-penny) nail.

So where did the penny system originate? Originally, it referred to the weight of nails per hundred.

SCREWS

Although there are four general categories of screws — drywall screws, production screws, wood screws and sheet-metal screws — woodworkers are usually interested only in the latter two types, wood and sheet-metal.

The main difference between wood and sheet-metal screws is the thread (the part on the shaft of the screw that digs itself into the wood). Whereas sheet-metal screws can, obviously, penetrate metal surfaces better, due to sharper threads, wood screws have a shallower thread designed for softer materials. Both types of screws are sold in the same general measurements.

Flathead screws are used most commonly for the flush surfaces they provide.

Wood screws often have bright zinc plating, but are also sold as galvanized, solid bronze, brass, stainless steel or aluminum. They're sold almost everywhere.

Sheet-metal screws can be used to attach hardware in the woodshop, or to attach anything to metal.

You also may encounter medium-density fiberboard (MDF) screws, which do not have tapered bodies like wood screws, but have sharp threads useful in particleboard and MDF projects.

Screws usually are sold in lengths rang-

PENNY SIZE	NAIL LENGTH
2d	1"
3d	$1\frac{1}{4}$"
4d	$1\frac{1}{2}$"
5d	$1\frac{3}{4}$"
6d	2"
7d	$2\frac{1}{4}$"
8d	$2\frac{1}{2}$"
9d	$2\frac{3}{4}$"
10d	3"
12d	$3\frac{1}{4}$"
16d	$3\frac{1}{2}$"
20d	4"

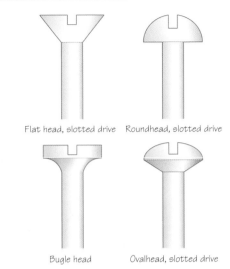

Flat head, slotted drive   Roundhead, slotted drive

Bugle head   Ovalhead, slotted drive

COMMON WOOD SCREW HEAD OPTIONS

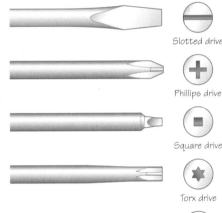

Slotted drive

Phillips drive

Square drive

Torx drive

Hex drive

COMMON SCREW AND BOLT DRIVE TYPES

ing from $\frac{1}{4}$" to 3" or 4". The diameter of the screw is referred to by a gauge number. The combinations of screw lengths and gauges that you can buy are almost infinite. You would order a screw like this: "Please give me a $\frac{1}{4}$" No. 3 screw." The inches refers to the length, and the number refers to the diameter size.

Screws numbered 0 are 0.060" in diameter; 1s are 0.073"; 2s are 0.086"; and so on, up to screw number 24 which is 0.372" in diameter.

BOLTS

A bolt is basically a metal rod that fastens objects together. It has a head at one end and a screw thread at the other, and it's secured by a nut.

Bolts aren't often used in fine furniture projects, or many woodworking projects in general, but they do show up in the shop now and then, in the form of shop equipment assemblies and the like.

Machine bolts are either threaded all the way to the head or, most often, have an unthreaded shank.

Machine bolts are referred to by their diameter and length, the number of threads per inch, the material they're made of and the type of head they have. Note that bolts' lengths are taken from the end of the bolt only to the underside of the head, not to the top.

All bolts come in coarse, fine or extra-fine threads — with coarse threads suitable for most woodshop applications.

Machine bolts range in size from 1" (with a diameter of 0.0730") up to 12" (with a diameter of 0.2160"), available in coarse or fine threads.

Carriage bolts have round tops with a square shank underneath to prevent the bolt from coming undone from that side. Carriage bolts are sold in lengths ranging from 1" to 8".

Washers, which are made of steel, are used as a protective measure between the head and a project's finished surface. They are sold according to hole diameter, ranging from $1/4$" to $1^3/16$".

BRACKETS, STANDARDS AND PINS

Brackets are described in the same section as nails, screws and bolts because they have one thing in common: They hold things.

Brackets, standards, clips and pins are used mostly for connecting shelving.

Standards, which are slotted and attach to the case's sides, come in a variety of materials and colors, such as zinc-plated, white-epoxy-coated, brass-finished, heavy-duty steel, or in a variety of hardwoods. Clips or brackets are inserted into the standards' slots. Brackets can handle heavier loads than clips.

Fixed brackets come in wood or metal, attach directly to a case or to a wall, and are often more ornamental in nature, in contrast to the rather utilitarian nature of standards.

Wood brackets come in classical, plain styles, as well as in a variety of decorative styles that are often used in home interiors.

Shelf pins are usually metal or plastic and are set in short holes. The shelving sits on the pins for support.

You can design your own, or buy, jigs to help you space your shelf-pin holes accurately. Shelf pins commonly come in $1/4$" or 5mm sizes.

Shelf pins can be used to support wooden and glass shelves. Pins are installed in holes that are drilled in the sides of the cabinets. Shown left to right, the first is a $1/4$" shelf support pin with a bracket. The hole in the bracket can be used to secure the shelf to the pin with a screw, or rubber cushions can be inserted that will hold a glass shelf in place. Next is a 5mm pin that will hold a tremendous amount of weight. Finally, a 7mm pin with a collar. The collar is installed in the hole and the pin is inserted. This pin setup adds a decorative element and the collar adds extra support for the pin when using softwoods like pine.

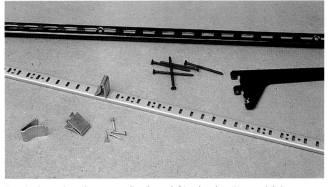

Standards are slotted to accept clips (lower left) or brackets (center right). The standards can be mounted flush by setting them into a groove in the cabinet's sides.

carriage bolt   lag bolt

machine bolt   machine bolt, fully threaded

COMMON BOLT TYPES

hinges

HINGES IN GENERAL

Hinges fall into one of two general categories: exposed or hidden. Exposed hinges, which are a bit easier to install, are very common and can be found at almost any hardware or home-improvement store. Hidden hinges, also called Eurohinges, have been, in the past, a little more difficult to find at the store, but they are gaining in popularity and are much more common these days and can be found in most home-improvement stores.

Exposed hinges are attached with screws to the outside of a face frame. Hidden hinges are attached with screws to the inside edge of a face frame. Both types are attached with screws to the inside face of the door.

While hinges usually fit into one of the above two categories, that's where the simplicity ends. There is an incredible array of hinge types, styles and applications.

BUTT HINGES

BUTT HINGES

The most common of all furniture hinges, butt hinges have been around since practically the beginning of modern woodworking, and come in many sizes. Basically, they are two leaves of metal joined together by barrels, or pivots, that allow them to open and close easily. One leaf is recessed into the cabinet, and the other leaf is recessed into the frame. The two leaves are folded together when the cabinet door is closed.

Butt hinges are referred to at the store by their length and width when fully open. So, a 2×1 butt hinge is 2" long and opens fully to 1".

Butt hinges, often sold in brass, aren't always plain Janes. They come with finial tips, ball tips and other fancy adornments that give them a certain elegance.

Piano hinges are a type of butt hinge, only longer. They can be cut to size at most hardware outlets and, obviously designed for strength applications, are often available up to 6' in length.

KNIFE HINGES

Knife hinges are also common hinges in the woodworking world. Intended for hinges that don't need to be incredibly strong, knife hinges consist of two interlocking leaves that turn toward one another.

Designed to be mounted to the tops and bottoms of doors, knife hinges are inserted into a slot that has been routed into the top and bottom of a door. The hinge is then attached to both the door frame and the door with screws. These screws adjust to properly align the door on the frame. Knife hinges remain visible from the front or side of the cabinet.

EUROHINGES

Often referred to as Euro or European hinges, these hidden hinges are considered very classy and are gaining more and more in popularity. They are very easy to adjust, are often used in contemporary cabinetry and are completely hidden from view after installation.

EUROHINGES

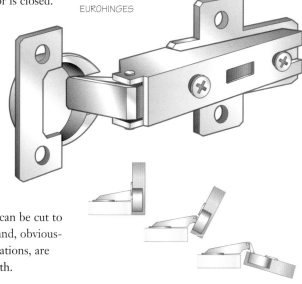

KNIFE HINGES

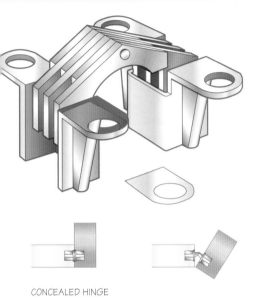

CONCEALED HINGE

CONCEALED HINGES

Concealed hinges are a particular brand of invisible hinge. These hinges do more than just allow doors to open and close; they let the furniture show without the unsightly hinge hardware getting in the way.

There are a variety of invisible hinges, including brass quadrant hinges that are ideal for smaller woodworking projects, like humidors and jewelry cases. There are also hinges for larger projects, as well as all-steel hinges for fire-rated doors.

OFFSET HINGE

Offset hinges are commonly used on kitchen cabinets or utility cabinets. The inside edges of the doors require a rabbet which creates a lip. The mounting plate of the hinge fits into the lip and wraps around the inside of the door. The other plate is attached to the face of the cabinets. These hinges are available in a $^3/_8$" (as shown in the illustration) or a $^3/_4$" offset (which requires no rabbet).

DROP-LEAF HINGES

Drop-leaf hinges have a special application. One side of the hinge is longer than the other in order to put the hinge out of view when a table leaf is lowered. This also makes it easier to clean the table and not get crumbs in the barrel of the hinge. These hinges aren't swaged, so they can be attached directly to the bottom of the table without mortising.

TO SWAGE OR NOT TO SWAGE

Butt hinges come in two different configurations as to how they close. In the illustration below (in the lower right corner of the page), the hinge on the right is typical of continuous hinges and most butt hinges for cabinetry. The leaves of the hinges at the barrel are not bent, so the hinge closes with the leaves separated. If this hinge were mounted directly on the cabinet and the door, there would be a gap the thickness of the hinge barrel between the door and the cabinet side. A mortise is needed to set the hinge in so the gap between the door and the cabinet side is less than the

PIVOT HINGE

DROP-LEAF HINGES

thickness of the hinge.

The hinge on the left in the illustration has been swaged, which means one leaf has been bent at the barrel so the leaves come together when the hinge is closed. This can eliminate the need for cutting a mortise for the hinge when it is mounted on the cabinet.

The hinges for room doors are usually swaged so the doors can be closed with a small gap at the hinge side and the door won't bind.

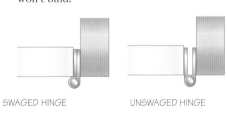

SWAGED HINGE   UNSWAGED HINGE

the euro or 32mm system

For several decades, European cabinetmakers have used a system of cabinetmaking that is quick, flexible and efficient.

The cabinet parts are cut out, edge-banded, drilled as needed for hardware and finished. Then the drawer hardware and hinge plates are installed. One of the benefits of this system is that the cabinet parts can be shipped flat and delivered to the job site. The cabinets can then be assembled and installed.

It's called the 32mm system because the 5mm hardware mounting holes are drilled in a line 32mm on center. Two vertical rows of these 5mm holes are drilled on the inside of the cabinet side panels. The side panels have 8mm assembly holes drilled near the top and bottom edges. Matching 8mm holes are drilled into the edges of the bottom and top panels. The drawer boxes are predrilled for dowels or assembly screws.

All the necessary hardware for this construction system can be found at home-improvement centers. The door hinges come in two parts: the hinge and its mounting plate. The drawer slides also come in two parts: the main part of the slide, which is mounted on the inside of the cabinet, and the drawer-box part, which is mounted on the drawer.

Special, deep-thread confirmat assembly screws are used to hold the cabinets together. These screws are 4mm, 5mm, 8mm and 10mm in diameter and come in 10mm to 50mm lengths. A special stepped drill is available for drilling the 8mm and 10mm assembly screws. It countersinks, counterbores and drills a pilot hole, all at the same time!

Adjustable leveling feet can be mounted on the bottom of the cabinet. These are used to level the cabinets when they are installed and are adjusted with a screwdriver from the inside of the cabinet through a small hole drilled in the bottom of the cabinet. After the cabinets have been leveled and set, these holes are plugged with plastic covers. The feet also have clips that will accept cleats mounted on the cabinet base fronts. The base is simply pushed and clipped into place after the cabinets have been installed.

Hardware is available for hanging and leveling the wall cabinets. A hanger rail is attached level on the wall, cleats are attached to the back of the wall cabinet and then the cabinet is hung by these cleats on the rail. If front-to-back or end-to-end leveling is needed, access holes drilled in the back of the cabinet allow adjustment of the hanging cleats with a screwdriver. These holes are then plugged with plastic covers.

For connecting multiple cabinets together, connector nuts are available. Aligned holes are drilled through the sides of the cabinets to be connected, then the connector nut is inserted through the two cabinets and screwed together. It's a two-part connector, with an internally threaded sleeve and a machine bolt that screws into the sleeve. The two parts have flat heads, making it a very solid connector that won't let the cabinets slip out of alignment with each other.

Face frames are sometimes used with the European system. The frames can be built and finished separately, then put on the cabinets at final assembly. They are attached with glue and dowels, biscuits or pocket-hole screws inserted from the inside of the cabinet into the back of the face frame.

The drawer boxes are assembled using 8mm dowels or confirmat screws (with plastic covers for the screw heads). Then the drawer slides are attached to the boxes. All drawer slides come in two parts — one that mounts on the drawer box and one that mounts on the inside of the cabinet.

A variety of options is available for drawer slides. Three-quarter extension slides (which let the drawer be pulled out about three-quarters of the depth of the drawer box) mount on the bottom of the sides of the drawer box. Full-extension slides mount on the sides of the drawer boxes. An undermount full-extension slide is also available (this slide is not seen when the drawer is opened). All of the cabinet parts of these slides are attached using 5mm by 10mm Euro or 32mm system screws in the 5mm holes.

The drawer-box face panels have 25mm-diameter by 13mm-deep holes drilled into their backs to accept adjustable inserts used to mount the drawer faces to the drawer boxes. A machine screw is inserted into this hardware through the drawer-box front. After the drawers are put into the cabinet, these screws are snugged up and the drawer faces can be adjusted as needed. Permanent screws are then added to hold the faces in place.

The cabinet doors are drilled with 35mm-diameter by 13mm-deep holes for the hinges. The hinges are pressed or set into place with two screws. After the cabinets have been installed, the doors are hung by clipping the hinges into place on the hinge plates. The door hinges can be adjusted with a screwdriver to line up the doors on the cabinets.

Shelf pins or supports are available in several colors and styles. Brass- or silver-colored metal spoon-shaped pins fit into 5mm-, 8mm- and $1/4$"-diameter holes. These pins are very strong and work well for bookcases.

Plastic shelf pins are available for lighter-duty applications. There are also right-angle metal supports for glass shelves.

The backs of the cabinets are attached with screws, nails or staples driven into rabbets in the back edges of the side panels. The sides, bottoms, tops, shelves, bases, top rails (used on the base cabinets), doors and drawer-box front panels are $5/8$" to $3/4$", or 16mm to 19mm thick. The back panels, drawer-box sides, fronts, backs and bottoms are $1/2$" or 13mm thick. Sometimes $1/4$"- or 6mm-thick material is used for drawer bottom panels.

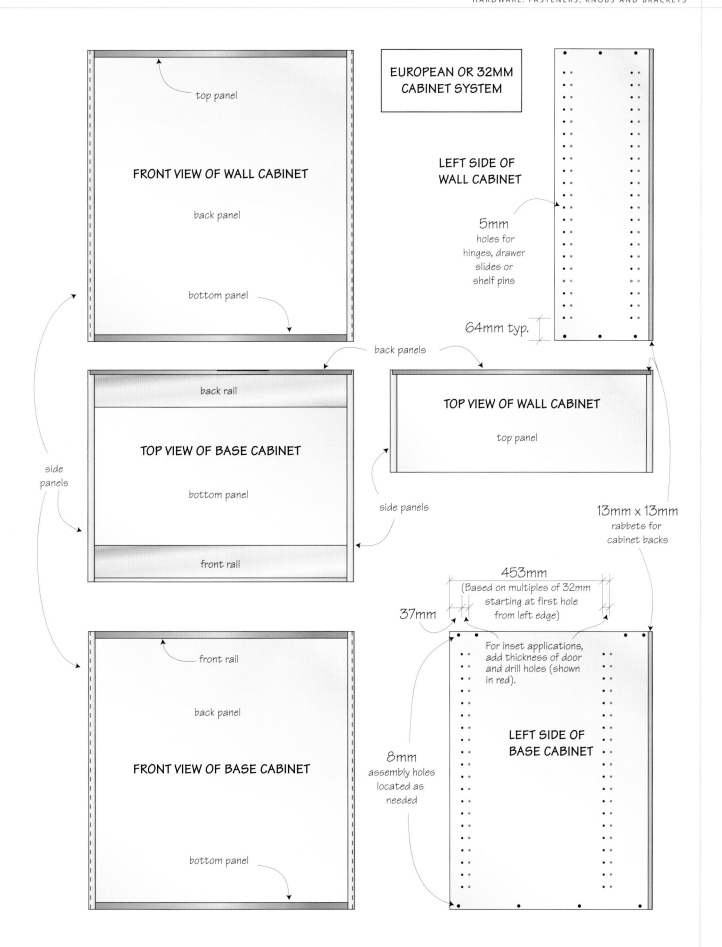

FRONT VIEW OF WALL CABINET

top panel

back panel

bottom panel

EUROPEAN OR 32MM
CABINET SYSTEM

LEFT SIDE OF
WALL CABINET

5mm
holes for
hinges, drawer
slides or
shelf pins

64mm typ.

back panels

TOP VIEW OF BASE CABINET

back rail

bottom panel

front rail

side
panels

TOP VIEW OF WALL CABINET

top panel

side panels

13mm x 13mm
rabbets for
cabinet backs

FRONT VIEW OF BASE CABINET

front rail

back panel

bottom panel

453mm
(Based on multiples of 32mm
starting at first hole
from left edge)

37mm

For inset applications,
add thickness of door
and drill holes (shown
in red).

LEFT SIDE OF
BASE CABINET

8mm
assembly holes
located as
needed

moulding styles

Mouldings are used to add decoration to cabinets and furniture. On built-in bookcases and furniture, mouldings are used to cover the gaps between the walls and the edges of the built-ins. This fits the built-in to the walls and gives a decorative finish to the installation.

Mouldings come in hundreds of shapes and profiles and can be milled from any species of wood.

CROWN MOULDING

Crown moulding is used mainly as decoration and ornamentation in rooms. It is installed where the wall meets the ceiling, creating a stylish transition from the wall to the ceiling. When bookcases are built into a room, crown moulding can be used to fit the bookcase to the ceiling, or it can be attached to the top of the bookcase, even if the bookcase doesn't go all the way to the ceiling. Crown moulding can also add the final touch to an armoire or media center.

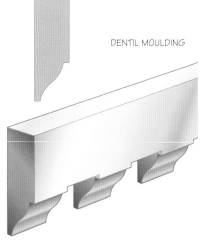

DENTIL MOULDING

CROWN MOULDING COMBINED WITH DENTIL MOULDING

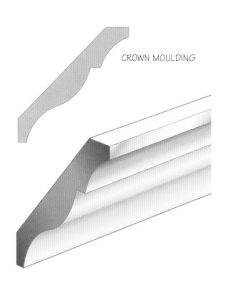

CROWN MOULDING

DENTIL MOULDING

Dentil moulding can be used to add interest and movement to an otherwise plain-looking room or piece of furniture. The moulding is usually installed under the edge of a top, around the sides of a cabinet or at the corner where a wall meets a ceiling.

Dentil moulding can be used in combination with other mouldings to create a striking look. For example, if dentil moulding is combined with crown moulding, a formal look can be achieved, which greatly enhances the look of any room or piece of furniture. Experimenting with different combinations of mouldings can yield some exciting results!

PICTURE MOULDING

There are about as many styles of picture moulding as the imagination can think of, and many of the most popular styles are available in home-improvement centers.

As with other mouldings, by using picture mouldings in combination with one another, many "new" mouldings can be created. If, however, the exact profile or wood type of any picture (or any variety) moulding cannot be found, many styles of router bits are available for you to create your own moulding in any wood type you like.

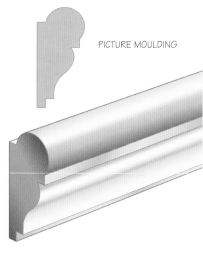

PICTURE MOULDING

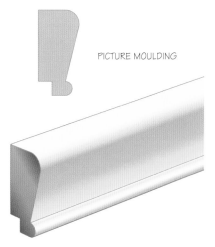

PICTURE MOULDING

BED RAIL BRACKETS

There are two common ways to hold the side rails, footboard and headboard of a bed together. One is by using bed bolts, which are installed by drilling holes into the legs of the bed and inserting the bolts into the ends of the side rails, which have matching holes drilled into their ends. The bolt is screwed into a captured nut in the end of the side rail. The bolt holes in the legs are usually covered with a brass decorative plate that swings open and closed.

The other method of putting a bed together is by using a two-part bracket. The female part of the bracket is set into a mortise in the legs, and the male part is set into the ends of the side rails. The male part usually has two hooks that interlock with slots in the female part. This is the easiest way to put together and take apart a bed, and this hardware is very strong.

Older beds had similar hardware. The male part in the rails was a $\frac{1}{8}$"-thick piece of stamped steel with two hooks. The legs had a corresponding slot housing two steel pins that interlocked with the hooks on the side rails. This hardware is harder to find; usually the bed manufacturer will have to be contacted to get replacement parts.

CASTERS AND FURNITURE GLIDES

If you have a heavy cabinet or piece of furniture, sometimes it's good to mount casters on the bottom of the piece. Castors come in sizes ranging from 1"- to 5"-diameter wheels. Depending on the floor surface (carpet, concrete, wood or tile), different types of wheel materials are available that will make moving the piece easier and not harm the floor. Smooth nylon, plastic or steel wheels are good to use on carpet. If you have a heavy piece of machinery, 3"- to 5"-diameter steel wheels can make it a breeze to move. There is a lot less friction because the wheels are so hard.

Special furniture castors are available. They're round with a roller built into the wheel and come with steel wheels with no tread or with a rubber-coated wheel that works very well on hardwood floors. These castors come in a variety of colors, including brass, chrome and black.

Glides are used when a piece of furniture needs to be elevated very slightly off the floor or when a cabinet needs to be leveled.

Furniture glides are available in steel, rubber and hard nylon. They can be adjustable steel feet with a threaded rod that inserts into a T-nut. Rubber and nylon glides come with a nail shank that is simply driven into the bottom of a leg or cabinet. Steel glides with three prongs are available for very little cost. These are hammered into the bottoms of legs or a cabinet.

DRAWER SLIDES

Fitted drawers are exactly that: The drawer is the same size as the cabinet opening and is fitted to that opening using no hardware. But for the rest of us who don't fit drawers, a huge variety of drawer slides is available.

FULL-EXTENSION DRAWER SLIDES

Full-extension drawer slides allow the drawer box to be opened completely and are most commonly mounted on the sides of the drawer box. These slides are rated from light duty to very heavy duty (file or tool) drawers. These slides have ball-bearing runners that will last for years. Undermount versions of full-extension slides are available. All side-mount slides require the drawer box to be built 1" smaller than the opening it goes into.

The photo above shows full-extension, side-mounting drawer slides. These are interchangeable for left or right drawer sides.

These are three-quarter-extension drawer slides. These are very durable and available at any home-improvement center. They are labeled left and right. The right drawer runner captures the roller of the cabinet runner which keeps the drawer centered.

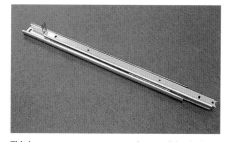

This is a two-part, center-mount drawer glide. The bottom part is attached to the front and back rails of the drawer opening in the cabinet. The upper part is attached to the bottom of the drawer with the vertical bracket wrapping up the back of the drawer box.

Furniture glides come in a huge assortment. Glides are great for leveling and moving furniture. They also protect floors and carpets. Clockwise starting at upper left are adjustable leveling feet (installed using T-nuts); nylon glides with rubber cushions; nylon glides with swivels; nylon glides with felt feet; nylon glides; and metal feet with rubber cushions.

THREE-QUARTER EXTENSION DRAWER SLIDES

Three-quarter extension drawer slides allow the drawer box to be opened about two-thirds to three-quarters of its depth. These slides are rated light to medium duty and operate very quietly and smoothly. They are epoxy-coated in white, almond and dark brown. They have indents that prevent the drawer from being pulled out without first lifting slightly on the front of the drawer. These slides are most commonly used in kitchens and desks.

UNDERMOUNT DRAWER SLIDES

Undermount drawer slides are a good choice when you don't want to see the hardware. Also, the drawer box can be made almost the same size as the opening it goes into. Two basic undermount styles are available: a single monorail center-mount slide and a two-rail system.

FLIPPER-DOOR SLIDES

Entertainment centers have become a standard piece of furniture in a lot of homes. Flipper doors (doors that slide into pockets in the sides of the cabinet) have become the door of choice for these pieces of furniture. Flipper-door hardware comes with two full-extension slides and two Euro-hinges. The slides are mounted to the sides of the cabinet, and the hinges are mounted to the door. When the door is opened to 90° it can be pushed straight back into the cabinet, out of the way, giving everyone a clear view of the television in the cabinet.

All of the above slides are available at most large home-improvement centers.

KNOBS AND PULLS

After you've built your furniture or cabinetry, now is the time choose the hardware that will help you open and close the doors and drawers. These are tough decisions: Too many choices are available in the decorative hardware world.

Knobs and pulls are available in wood, plastic, metal, glass, etc. A complete spectrum of colors and textures is also available.

The type of hardware you choose for your projects is purely subjective, but here are some basic guidelines: Knobs are generally used on smaller-faced drawers and doors. Pulls are used on larger drawers and doors. Of course, all this is up to you. Two knobs or pulls on large dresser drawers are acceptable, as are oversize knobs and pulls to achieve a special effect.

As a guide to choosing hardware, consider the type of materials used to make the project, the style and the size. How will the project be used? Does it match anything else in the room or the house? What color is it? You get the idea.

installing hardware

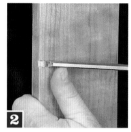

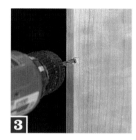

INSTALLING A RAT-TAIL HINGE

Back when I was making period furniture for a living, I got a lesson in installing rat-tail hinges. It started out like this: "You get one shot to install this hinge right." With that introduction, I got a lot of practice installing these hinges on expensive furniture.

Let's start with a little basic knowledge. These hinges work best on cabinets with face frames. There are three basic parts: the leaf, pintel (or pin) and the snipe, the piece that penetrates the stile

and is splayed like a cotter pin inside. Practice the mounting operation on scrap before mounting for real. Begin by placing the door in its opening and holding the hinge in the location where it will be mounted. Mark both sides of the snipe location on the stile (1). Next, using a small saw, cut in about $\frac{1}{4}$" across the grain at the marked lines. Using a $\frac{1}{4}$" chisel, clean out a small chamfer on the edge (2). This will give a flat surface for drilling a $\frac{1}{4}$" hole. Drill

a hole at about a 45° angle through the stile (3). With the entire hinge assembled, place the snipe in the hole. You might have to swage the snipe to get the hinge to seat properly. Do this in a vise with a hammer, while the pintel is still in place. When the hinge looks right, attach the pintel spade and the leaf (4). When you've got a good fit, hold the hinge in place and peen the snipe ends over after splaying them with a screwdriver (5).

INSTALLING A BUTT HINGE

The first photo shows a swaged butt hinge. The leaves have been peened at the barrel so they come together flat. This makes it possible to install this hinge without cutting a mortise. If it was installed without using a mortise, the gap between the door and cabinet side would be the thickness of the two plates when they are closed.

If you would like a smaller gap around the door, cut a mortise in the door the depth of one of the leaves of the hinge. Use a utility knife to score around the leaf of the hinge as shown (2). Then use a chisel or router to cut away the material in the scored area to the depth of the thickness of one leaf (3). This will give you a gap around the door the thickness of a single leaf. Butt hinges that are not swaged need to be mortised. The depth of the mortise will determine the gap around the door. Step 4 shows how the hinge should seat in the mortise.

INSTALLING A KNIFE HINGE

Begin by centering the hinge on the door. Using a router set up with a straight-cutting bit and a fence, cut the mortise for the hinge (1). Square out the corners with a chisel (2). Use the same router setup and cut the mortise in the bottom and top of the cabinet (3). This is easily done if the mortises are cut before final assembly of the cabinet. If the cabinet is assembled first, the mortises will need to be cut using a chisel. That is more difficult, but many craftsmen choose to do it that way. These hinges provide a very neat and clean appearance to the final project and are well worth the time and effort needed to install them. There is no room for error in the installation because the doors cannot be adjusted after the hinges are installed.

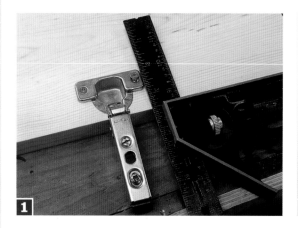

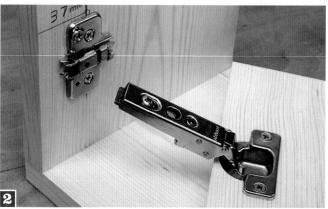

INSTALLING A EUROPEAN HINGE

All European hinges are installed using a flat-bottomed 35mm-diameter hole (a $1^{3}/_{8}$"-diameter hole works also) drilled $^{1}/_{8}$" to $^{3}/_{16}$" from the edge of the door. The hinge should be installed square to the edge of the door (1). The mounting plate for the hinge is installed on the interior side of the cabinet 37mm on center from the front edge of the cabinet (2). This is the most common mounting for these hinges. When the door is closed, it will overlay the front of the cabinet (3). If an inset door is needed, the mounting plate holes are drilled 56mm on center from the front edge of the cabinet. The hinges are adjustable up, down, in, out and side-to-side up to 4.5mm (approximately $^{3}/_{16}$").

INSTALLING A FLUSH-MOUNTING HINGE AND CATCH

Locate the lid or door on the box or cabinet. Then draw a line that shows the center location of the hinge. Put the hinge in place (1). Drill a hole and install the center screw in the box. Then do the same for the center hole in the lid. Install the second hinge the same way. If the lid works fine and it lines up after being opened and closed a couple of times, install the rest of the mounting screws (2).

Installing a catch is the same as installing the hinges. Close the lid, draw a center line or center the catch on the box. Attach the bottom part of the catch (3). Line up the top part of the catch by closing it over the lower part. Then attach the top part (4).

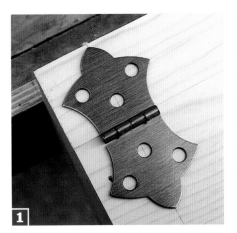

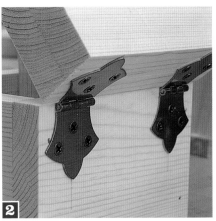

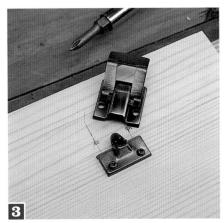

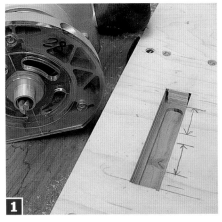

INSTALLING BED RAIL HARDWARE

Bed rail hardware makes it possible to quickly tear down and set up a bed. When properly installed, this hardware is strong and keeps the bed sturdy.

Begin by making a routing template that will guide a router set up with a guide bushing. Rout a slot in the bedpost that is the same width and depth as the plate of the bed rail hardware (1). Use a chisel to square the corners of the slot (2). Rout two clearance slots for the male half of the hardware (3). Repeat the above steps for installing the female hardware in the rail (4). Installing this hardware just a little below the surface of the wood will ensure the end of the rail will fit tightly against the bedpost.

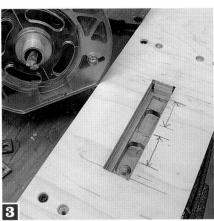

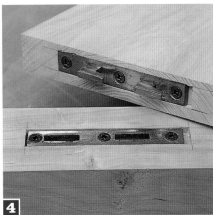

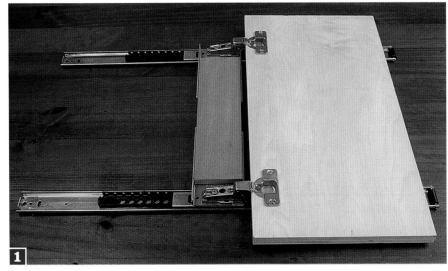

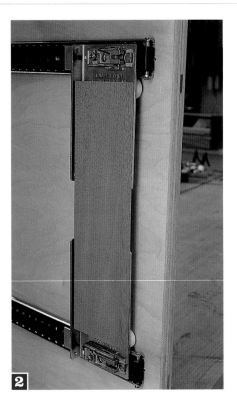

1

2

Pocket-door hardware uses two slides, two European hinges, two plates to which a keeper strip is installed and two sets of alignment rollers. The keeper strip holds the two hinges in alignment with each other (1). The slide assembly is installed on the inside of the cabinet side (2). When the door is attached, it can be pulled towards the front of the cabinet and closed like any other door. (These doors are inset.) When the door is opened 90° it can then be pushed towards the back of the cabinet, hidden from view. There are alignment rollers installed on the top and the bottom of the cabinet to keep the retracted door in the open position. Usually a false side is installed parallel to the cabinet side which creates a pocket that houses the open door. This hardware is great for entertainment centers.

A continuous hinge doesn't require a mortise to be installed in most cases. The barrel of the hinge conceals the gap between the door and the cabinet. When installing a lid using this hinge, a mortise is needed to close the gap between the box's top edge and the lid.

A right-angle knife hinge is installed the same as a straight knife hinge, with the addition of the angle.

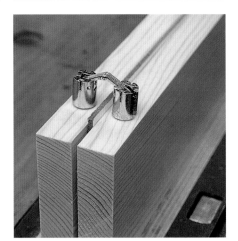

Hidden hinges are ideal for bifold doors. The hinges shown in the photo are installed by drilling two holes centered in the doors. Other styles of hidden hinges require a mortise, which is simply an elongated hole.

⊙ ANN ROCKLER JACKSON, MAYOR OF ROCKLERVILLE

Most woodworkers know Rockler Woodworking and Hardware.

But not as well as Ann Rockler Jackson, whose father, Nordy Rockler, founded the company in 1954.

"It's a real honest profession, selling the tools so people can build things," she said.

When Ann first started, it was a much smaller company. There were only 7 employees at the time, and there are now over 350 employees at Rockler.

"Through osmosis, I know quite a bit about woodworking," she said, adding that her father built all of her family's furniture when she was growing up. "I know what good construction is."

As the cover of the Rockler catalog says, "Welcome to Rocklerville: Home of 5,000 Woodworking Products."

For woodworkers everywhere, the Rockler catalog is a joy to receive in the mail. You feel like a kid, weeks before Christmas, poring over the toy section of the JCPenney gift catalog.

Inside the Rockler catalog's pages, you'll find an incredible range of woodworking items, such as project plans, books, table legs, deck accessories, Arts & Crafts furniture trim, knobs, pulls, door accessories, drawer glides, hinges, gardening tools, screws, router bits, power tools, clamps, jigs and more.

And, of course, if you have Internet access, you don't even have to wait for your new catalog. You can just surf and order at www.rockler.com.

Though not a full-time woodworker, Ann designs furniture and has built several projects, including a dictionary stand from a "big piece of oak" through her local community education program.

"I've been here for 32 years," said Ann, who quit college at one point just because she loved working at her dad's company so much.

She eventually did go back to college, and is now close to having her master's degree in, fittingly, decorative arts.

"Of course, we weren't allowed to take woodworking in high school," she laughed. "I could take classes in home economics, though."

One of the things Ann likes about woodworking is the fact that it's not a static occupation; it's always changing, with new techniques and new tools coming out all the time.

One of Ann's projects has been to start up womeninwoodworking.com, a great source of information for both men and women of every experience level to find and share information about woodworking.

"It's a service-oriented site, not a marketing-oriented site," explained Ann. "The

Ann Rockler Jackson, CEO of Rockler Woodworking

forum is one of the best forums out there, and men feel comfortable visiting it, too."

Not surprisingly, Ann is most intrigued by some of the hardware that is used to build furniture. The quality of the drawer pulls, knobs and hinges that are used in a particular project definitely catch her trained eye.

"I'm pretty fussy about the hardware that is used on a woodworking project. Some people might like nice jewelry; I like really good drawer slides!"

Women in woodworking

This is the logo of the womeninwoodworking.com Web site.

> shop math
circles, squares and measurements

Even the mere mention of the word *math* can send chills up and down the spines of the most hardened and experienced woodworkers. But in fact, most woodworkers know and use math more than they realize.

Woodworkers add and subtract fractions, figure board footage, calculate angles and, of course, tally up how much all that lumber is actually going to cost.

This chapter contains some ideas, formulas and charts that will help you understand how shop math can make your work go easier and quicker.

These are the basics you need: how to read a ruler, add, subtract, multiply and divide. Using a small shop calculator can help with processing more numbers than you can handle in your head or on paper.

So, got your pencils poised and your calculators warmed up? Let's get started!

the basics

READING A RULER

It may seem redundant to talk about how to read a ruler, but just so we're on the same page we'll take a quick look.

In the United States woodworkers use inches for measuring. On an inch ruler, inches are divided into halves, then half of those and half again and again and sometimes, again. This last division would be 32nds of an inch. Most woodworkers will work to an accuracy of 16ths of an inch. There are 12 inches in a foot and 3 feet in a yard.

In Europe and other places in the world, the metric system of measurement is used. Reading a metric ruler is a little different from reading an inch ruler in that all divisions are done in 10s. The smallest unit is a millimeter, then centimeter, decimeter and meter.

PLANE GEOMETRY

Of all the types of math there are, plane geometry is probably the most used in the woodshop. Squares and circles fall into this type of math. A square or rectangle has four sides. How much material would you need for a picture frame? Measuring around the outside of the frame will give you the length of material you would need. Or, because opposite sides are the same length, 2 times the length plus 2 times the width will give you this same length of material needed.

Geometry divides a circle into 360°. Measuring in angles and lengths will give you the tools needed to build 90 percent of your projects. To figure the angle between the sides of a box or frame with sides of equal lengths, divide 360 by the number of sides. A four-sided box would have each side at 90° to its adjoining sides. To find the miter angle that you need to cut to create this angle, divide the joint angle by 2.

TRIGONOMETRY

Trigonometry is another system of math that can help you in the shop. The basis

for this system is the right triangle. A right triangle has three parts: a side (a), a base (b) and a hypotenuse (c). One angle (C) is always 90° and the sum of the other two angles always totals 90°. The formula that we all learned in *The Wizard of Oz* when the Tin Man got his brain is $A^2 + B^2 = C^2$. This is the Pythagorean theorem. A long time ago, a Greek philosopher named Pythagoras figured it all out. How does this apply to woodworking? You can make a triangle on any piece where you need to know the length of a particular side, then apply the formula to get the length of that side. (You need to know the length of the two other sides.)

But wait, there's more. There is a proportional relationship between the angles at the corners and the other parts of the right triangle. Words like sine, cosine and tangent start popping up. Suffice it to say these proportional relationships can help you determine the length of any side or angle in a right triangle. All you need to know is the length of two sides, or the length of one side and the angle of one corner. The chart "Trigonometry: Right Triangles" shows you the formulas you can use to do this.

Using these formulas will require finding squares and square roots. It is suggested that you buy a scientific calculator and use it to work these formulas. All the square root stuff is already figured out inside that little calculator and it will save

you lots of time.

Use trigonometry to make arcs and circles. See the formulas under circles and arcs in the chart.

If using all this math is a bit daunting for you, make full-scale measured drawings of any project that requires special angles, curves, or arcs. Then use the math to help you finalize and double-check dimensions.

If you have access to a computer and are willing to spend some time learning something new, computer-aided design (CAD) software will calculate all lengths, widths, angles, arcs and circles as you are drawing. When you get all the parts to fit together in the drawing, the software will give you all the final numbers you need to construct the project.

INCHES RULER

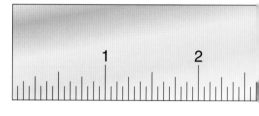

METRIC RULER

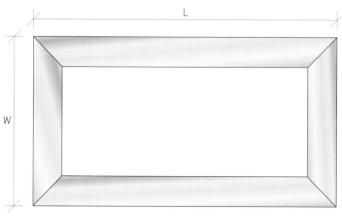

USING NUMBERS TO CREATE PROPORTIONAL BALANCE IN DESIGNING FURNITURE

Once again, let's turn to our old friend Pythagoras. He showed that the balance between form and function, which is the basis of nature's designs, is the result of precise mathematical relationships. Using mathematics to achieve the perfect proportion of one part to another in a structure, he came up with the Golden Section. It means that larger parts are proportional to smaller parts as those parts are proportional to even smaller parts. Not only that, the sum of the smaller parts is proportional to the larger. Expressed as a mathematical formula, which is foolproof, it reads: AC/CB = AB/AC. Expressed another way, the Golden Section equals .618 or its reciprocal 1.618. (See the drawing "The Golden Section" on the following page.)

This equation really does work and seems to be a naturally occurring principle in nature. The swirl in a conch shell has these same proportions as the larger diameter goes to smaller in different levels. It has been discovered that Bach, Beethoven and other composers wrote large phrases that were proportional to smaller themes that were contained within the larger phrase. A certain number of notes and a certain number of measures are found throughout their music that fit this equation. They were not conscious of this on one level, but it seems they were on a deeper level. The same is true for art and, of course, architecture. How does this apply to woodworking?

By being aware of how one part of a piece of furniture relates to the rest of the piece and parts of the piece you can create a project that will fit into the golden section and people will feel and sense the proportions more than they will know what they are seeing. It really happens.

The illustration "The Golden Section" on the following page shows how this equation works on a piece of furniture and

how you can adapt it to your own designs. When you've created a design you like, draw it out full scale or cut out full-scale cardboard parts that will give you a better sense of proportion in real-world terms.

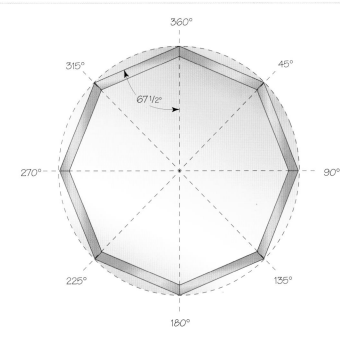

This illustration shows how a circle can be divided and the resulting angles. This can be applied to any number of divisions of the circle. To determine the cutting angle, divide the joint angle by 2.

$$R = \frac{(L \div 2)^2 + H^2}{2H}$$

Where:
L = the length of the arc,
H = the height of the arc, and
R = the radius of the arc

$$R = \frac{(18 \div 2)^2 + 2.125^2}{2 \times 2.125} = \frac{81 + 4.52}{4.25} = \frac{85.52}{4.25} =$$

20.122 or approx. $20^1/8"$

Length of arc (L)

18"

$2^1/8"$ is height of arc (H)

$20^1/8"$ radius (R)

You can find the radius of an arc if you know the length and height of the arc.

THE GOLDEN SECTION
(how it can be used in furniture design)

A   C   B

x + y = z
The drawer heights are based
on the Fibonacci number series,
where each successive number is the
sum of the two numbers preceeding it:
1, 1, 2, 3, 5, 8, 13, 21, 34, etc.

Golden Section equation is
AC/CB=AB/AC.
The value of the Golden Section is
.618 or its reciprocal 1.618.

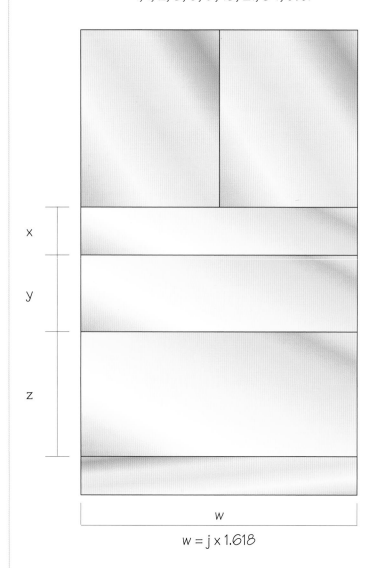

w = j x 1.618

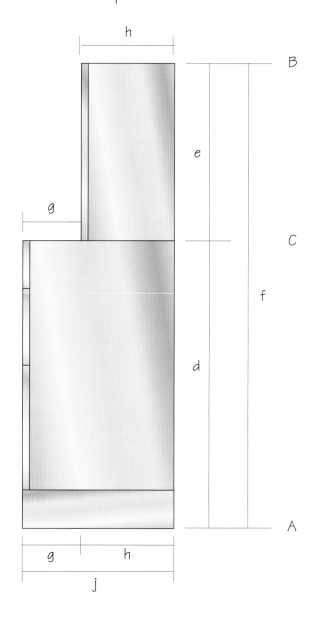

TRIGONOMETRY: RIGHT TRIANGLES

PARTS AND ANGLES KNOWN	FORMULAS FOR PARTS AND ANGLES TO BE FOUND		
Side a, base b	$c = \sqrt{a^2 + b^2}$	$tanA = a \div b$	$B = 90° - A$
Side a, hyp. c	$b = \sqrt{c^2 - a^2}$	$sinA = a \div c$	$B = 90° - A$
Base b, hyp. c	$a = \sqrt{c^2 - b^2}$	$sinB = b \div c$	$A = 90° - B$
Side a, angle A	$c = a \div sinA$	$b = a \div tanA$	$B = 90° - A$
Side a, angle B	$c = a \div cosB$	$b = a \times tanB$	$A = 90° - B$
Base b, angle A	$c = b \div cosA$	$a = b \times tanA$	$B = 90° - A$
Base b, angle B	$c = b \div sinB$	$a = b \div tanB$	$A = 90° - B$
Hyp. c, angle A	$b = c \times cosA$	$a = c \times sinA$	$B = 90° - A$
Hyp. c, angle B	$b = c \times sinB$	$a = c \times cosB$	$A = 90° - B$

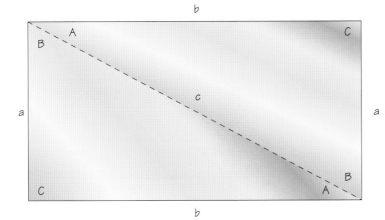

This drawing shows the relationship of opposing and adjacent angles when a rectangle is divided by a diagonal.

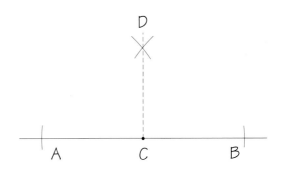

A compass can be used to do other things besides draw circles. As shown in these illustrations, drawing a line perpendicular (or square) to another line can be done easily. Set the compass to any radius, hold at point C and strike an arc at A then at B. Then, hold the compass at point A, then at point B, striking two arcs that intersect at D.

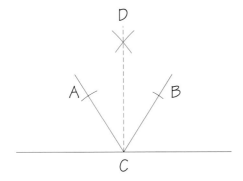

Bisect an angle by marking off points at A and B from C. Then, hold the compass at A and B, striking two intersecting arcs at D. Line CD will bisect angle ACB.

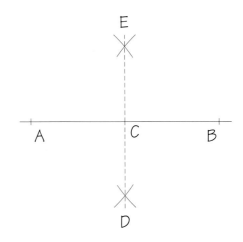

Find the midpoint of a line by holding the compass at A, then at B, drawing intersecting arcs at D and E. Line DE will intersect AB at its midpoint.

CIRCLES

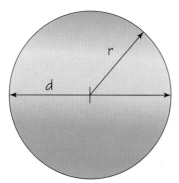

Circumference = 3.1416 x d
Area = 3.1416 x r²

RIGHT TRIANGLES

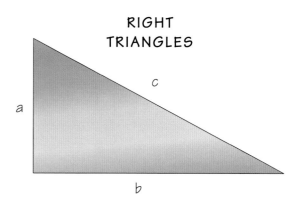

Perimeter = a + b + c
Area = (a x b) ÷ 2

RECTANGLES

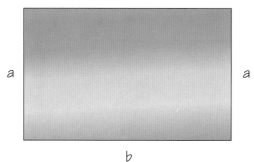

Perimeter = 2a + 2b
Area = a x b

ELLIPSES

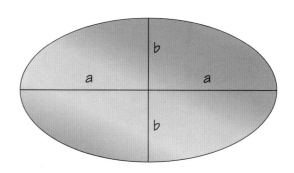

Circumference = 3.1416 (1.5 [a+b] - √ab)
Area = 3.1416 x a x b

POLYGONS (all sides equal lengths)
N = Number of sides

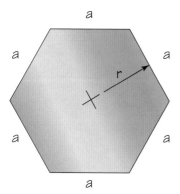

Perimeter = N x a
Area = (N x a x r) ÷ 2

CORNER ANGLES FOR POLYGONS
N = Number of angles

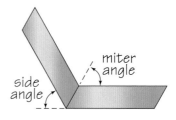

Side angle = 360 ÷ N
Miter angle = 90 - (360 ÷ 2N)

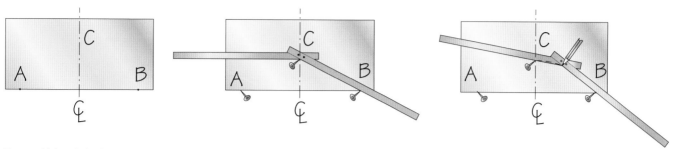

The arc stick is a tried and true method of striking an arc large or small.

1. Lay out the arc's end points (A and B) and the highest point (C). Put screws or nails at these points.

2. Use two sticks a little longer than the distance from A to B. Hold one stick against C and parallel to the bottom of your layout board and hold the other stick against C and B. Attach the sticks to one another.

3. Start drawing the arc with your pencil in the joint of the sticks. Hold this joint against A and move the sticks and pencil along all three points.

To draw an ellipse, all you need are a compass, two nails and a piece of string.

Start by drawing two lines, AB and CD, perpendicular to each other and intersecting at their centers.

AB is the final length and CD is the final width of the ellipse.

Set your compass to AX and hold the tip at D. Strike an arc at Y and Z on AB.

Put the nails at Y and Z.

Tie the string in a loop, holding it tight between Y, C (where you are centering your pencil) and Z.

Keep the string tight as you draw the ellipse.

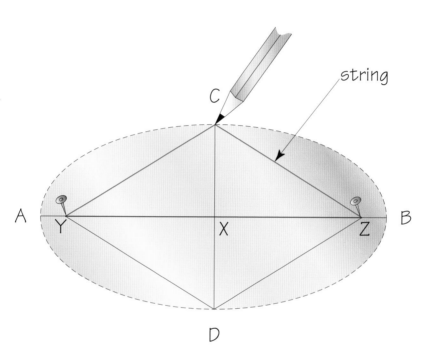

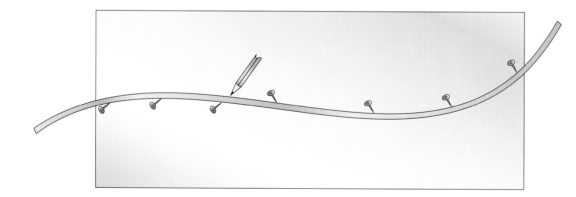

Many times it's easier to bend a thin strip of wood to the desired curve or curves, rather than trying to plot the radius or diameter. On compound curves (curves that have constantly changing or multiple radii), it is definitely easier. A $\frac{1}{4}$" × $\frac{1}{4}$" strip of wood or a $\frac{3}{16}$"- diameter hardwood dowel will bend nicely to most curves you will need to draw.

GREENE & GREENE'S 1907 BLACKER HOUSE STILL IMPRESSES AFICIONADOS

Although Greene & Greene's Gamble House is more often discussed in Arts & Crafts circles, the Greene brothers' Blacker House in Pasadena, California, has been garnering a lot of press and attention lately due to a recently released book.

Reviews of this architectural book have been popping up in such unlikely places as *People* magazine. It's been getting so much mainstream attention very likely because actor Brad Pitt took several atmospheric photographs that were included, but the Blacker House itself is deserving of paparazzi attention.

It's a gorgeous home oozing with the aura of the Arts & Crafts movement. Here is an excerpt from this interesting book.

GREENE & GREENE: THE BLACKER HOUSE

Authors: Randell L. Makinson, Hon. AIA, Thomas A. Heinz, AIA, and Brad Pitt

In the Blacker House of 1907, architects Charles and Henry Greene developed and brought forward the full thrust of their new and highly refined timber style to create what became the largest and most elaborate of their wooden masterworks.

Here they demonstrated the fundamental concepts of their Arts & Crafts philosophy: the provision of shade and shelter in a hot arid climate, free cross-circulation of air, and an open relationship between house and garden. This applied equally well to the large estate and to the modest bungalow, as manifested by the compatibility of the scale of the main Blacker House with the three outbuildings.

The Greenes designed a long timbered porte cochere that angled from the central entry and was supported by a massive clinker-brick pier in the island of the grand circular drive.

THE STRUCTURE

To Greene & Greene, it was important that the fundamental nature of the structure and the materials be honestly expressed on both the exterior and interior.

The feature that had impressed the brothers in the design of the Japanese Pavilion at the Chicago World Columbian Exposition in 1893 was the straightforward expression of the component parts of the structure — the posts, beams, rafters and skin (the wall panels) — used frankly. The inherent qualities of each part of the construction brought to the design its own appropriate color, texture and rhythm.

The careful attention to scale and proportion in the composition of these essential components made any kind of applied artificial decoration unnecessary.

The Blacker exterior states exactly what it is: a wood-timber structure in southern California, as fresh and forthright as a Japanese temple, as shingle-clad as the New England Shingle Style, and as lyrical in its massing and fenestration as the chalets of the Black Forest or the Swiss Alps.

And while it is all of these in spirit, it is none of these in reality, for the Greenes infused each new project with distinct regional considerations, looking first to climate, environment, materials available, and the habits and tastes of the owner as the initial determinants of their designs.

THE EXTERIOR

Built upon rugged clinker-brick foundations and broad terra-cotta-paved terraces, the powerful post-and-beam structure, with its brazen exploitation of metal-strap and wooden-dowel joinery, broad roof overhangs, projecting outriggers and rafter tails, provides a constant ballet of silhouettes and shadows as the sun moves through the day.

Within the strong and orderly design is a structural system with the opportunity for variation, which, under the Greenes' firm control, allowed them to infuse their designs with a relaxed flexibility. So they pushed, pulled, tucked or turned the composition when called upon to do so, without sacrificing either structural integrity or visual continuity.

By using color as a further differentiation between components, the architects brought to the composition another level of richness. Structural timbers, rafters and window trim were stained a medium dark brown; the redwood shakes of the exterior walls were green; and windows and doors were left a light natural finish.

Combined with the rich red-brown tones of the clinker-brick foundations,

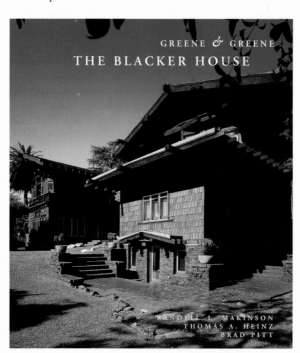

GREENE & GREENE
THE BLACKER HOUSE

RANDELL L. MAKINSON
THOMAS A. HEINZ
BRAD PITT

The *Greene & Greene: The Blacker House* book cover is shown at the left.

IMAGE COURTESY OF GIBBS SMITH, PUBLISHER

the slate gray-green of the composition rolled roofing, the rust of the metal-strapping details, and the multicolored imagery from the leaded-and-stained-glass windows, the Blacker House presented a lively and varied color palette.

The use of Cabot's transparent penetrating-oil stains was a critical factor in the Greene & Greene exterior color specification. The transparency of the stains allowed for the grain of the timbers and the varied coloration of the wood to respond differently to the stains.

This was especially effective on the split redwood shakes, where not only did the shakes differ in texture but also in color, resulting in a variation that gave the entire exterior a life and vitality that the flat uniformity of solid body stains and paints cannot duplicate.

THE ENTRY PORCH

To enter the Blacker House is to be subjected to a range of impressions. From the circular drive covered by the timber-

trussed porte cochere, the visitor ascends the broad brick stairs onto a Mission-tile entry porch that conveys a sense of intimacy, with its lower roof and the heavy timber trusses embracing the space.

In the evening, broad-hooded lanterns cast a soft glow across the terrace as the visitor follows the angle of the porch toward the tripartite bank of entry doors. Here, as in the Gamble House, the central door is wide and hospitable, and the lack of a screen promises an easy welcome.

THE MAIN HALL

As the visitor steps into the main hall, one is first welcomed by the warmth of the teak wall paneling and the lighting lanterns, and then is greeted by the long vista of the southern garden through the broad bank of clear-glass French doors opening onto the rear courtyard.

Overhead, the ceiling is of Douglas fir heavy-timber construction, and between the beams are panels of Port Orford cedar exhibiting a hint of difference between the transparent rubbed stains of the frames and the central panels.

Square pegs acknowledge the joinery of their construction and complete the hierarchy of Henry Greene's proportional relationships, which are essential to the grace of Greene & Greene designs.

Five hanging lanterns designed for the main hall softly illuminate, whether by day or evening, and despite the somewhat lim-

ited technology of the era in which they were created, become magical points of light, casting a warm glow around the space and across the grain of the hand-rubbed interior paneling.

Inez Peterson, who worked for the Blackers, recalled that "the wood all through the house is very smooth and satiny. Mr. Blacker usually stopped to rub his hands over it when going from one room to another."

In 1909, when Greene & Greene were designing the house in Berkeley for Nellie Blacker's sister, Caroline Canfield Thorsen, Mrs. J.W. Purchas, sister of William R. Thorsen, visited the just-completed Blacker House and wrote her brother her personal and sometimes humorous observations:

"Well I find the outside of the house and grounds very pretty and attractive but my impressions after moving through the various rooms was that the architect has let his fancy run riot in wood. There is so much wood about the outside that when one finds oneself encased in wooden rooms, wood walls, wood ceiling, wood floors, wood furniture, wood fixtures for light — well one has a little bit the feeling of a spider scrambling from one cigar box to another."

Randell L. Makinson is an architectural educator, historian and foremost authority on architects Greene & Greene. Thomas A. Heinz is a restoration architect, author and photographer. Brad Pitt is an actor, photographer and Greene & Greene aficionado.

This text is excerpted with permission from Gibbs Smith, Publisher, from the book Greene & Greene: The Blacker House *copyright © 2000, available from Gibbs Smith, Publisher (www.gibbs-smith.com).*

> dimensions
furniture design and measuring devices

Designing furniture involves much more than feverishly sketching an artistic form onto a scrap of paper, holding it up and shouting victoriously, "Yes! That's it! The most beautiful table anyone will ever build!"

Because no one will build that nifty new design you just created, not even you, unless you follow the most basic dimensions and standards that other woodworkers, through trial and error, have discovered make the most sense and result in the most sturdy, useful final projects.

In this chapter, you will learn about the most popular furniture styles that you can copy, how to dimension your project from a photograph, the standard dimensions of tables, chairs, beds, desks and shelves, as well as the variety of measuring devices that can help you map out your project.

furniture styles

If you're really ambitious, or just plain curious, you can track furniture styles back to the ornate Byzantine-era religious furniture or even back to the clunky, unstyled furniture of the Middle Ages. But most modern woodworkers stick to more recent influences, from about the 1700s on. Here are some brief descriptions of furniture styles you may choose to merely admire from afar, or implement into your own woodworking designs.

QUEEN ANNE STYLE

Queen Anne of England was in charge from 1702 until 1714, although the Queen Anne style of furniture was not influenced by her and actually incorporates furniture designed through the mid-1700s.

It's not an overly plain style, yet it avoids extreme statements or excessive decor. One telltale element of a Queen Anne furnishing is the use of the cabriole leg, which is utilitarian in its solid strength (although sometimes made thin and delicate), but also made attractive by its curves and pad feet.

You'll often see rosette and leaf carvings on Queen Anne furniture, as well as butterfly drawer pulls, finials and frontal veneers. This style was incredibly popular in America in the mid to late 1700s.

The Queen Anne style, in general, is marked by graceful lines and curves, and it often features furniture made of walnut, cherry or maple woods.

CHIPPENDALE STYLE

Thomas Chippendale, who lived from 1718 to 1779, was an English cabinetmaker and woodcarver whose furniture designs blended the Queen Anne style with more radical elements, such as Chinese influences. His style became very popular with the wealthy and with Americans after he published a trade catalog, *Gentleman and Cabinet Maker's Director*, in 1754, which also led to a string of imitators.

Queen Anne elements of Chippendale furniture include use of the cabriole leg, as well as ball-and-claw feet and fancier French rococo carving elements. Chinese Chippendale furniture was very different from the other furniture he designed, and somewhat modern in appearance, with geometric frameworks in chair backings.

Due to his carving background, Chippendale enjoyed utilizing mahogany in his furniture. Job Townsend and John Goddard are two names that stand out in American furniture design, and they implemented many Chippendale elements into their works.

SHERATON STYLE

Another English furniture designer, Thomas Sheraton, Jr., who lived from 1751 until 1806, designed pieces similar to his designing predecessor George Hepplewhite. The Hepplewhite and Sheraton styles are very similar, and borrowed heavily from Greek and Roman classical motifs.

Sheraton's style differed with his creative blending of utilitarian and aesthetically pleasing elements, in pieces like his twin beds, small tables and shaving mirrors.

Chairs designed by Sheraton also had rectangular backs and down-sloping armrests, and most of his furniture implemented decorative elements of the neoclassical movement, as well as French influences.

He published a four-volume book set, called *Cabinet-Maker and Upholsterer's Drawing Book*, in 1794.

ARTS & CRAFTS STYLE

Falling at the tail end of the Victorian Age's historic revival furniture, which enjoyed popularity from about 1830 until shortly after the turn of the century, Arts & Crafts furniture gained momentum partially in opposition to the opulent and somewhat frivolous Victorian furniture.

Arts & Crafts furniture, sometimes categorized as Craftsman or Mission furniture, was a movement and a style focusing on the importance of simple, handmade furniture, spearheaded by William Morris in England and Gustav Stickley in the U.S. Often made of oak, Arts & Crafts furniture includes square designs, exposed mortise-and-tenon joinery, slat backs and, sometimes, leather upholstery.

FEDERAL STYLE

British and American furniture styles weren't very different until the obvious division that occurred as a result of the American Revolution. As a result of that time period, American cabinetmakers and furniture designers began creating their own styles. Popular furniture of that time, from about 1790 until about 1830, actually was related to Hepplewhite and Sheraton furniture and displayed many neoclassical elements, with a French-American twist. As the French were assisting in the Revolution, and high-profile Americans such as John Adams and Benjamin Franklin were spending months at a time in Paris, French culture became very hip in America.

SHAKER STYLE

Shakers located to the United States in the late 1700s and established early settlements in New York, New England and the Midwest. Austere and utilitarian in nature, due to the strict religious beliefs of the Shaker people, Shaker furniture is now ironically very sought after and admired in general society. Its beauty lies in its simplicity.

Simple lines, elegant turnings, plain feet and oval boxes are characteristic of Shaker furnishings. Made mostly of pine and maple, Shaker furniture also consists of cane-seat ladderback chairs, simple candle wall sconces, tall cupboards or chests with wooden knobs, as well as clocks, tables, dressers and desks.

It seems to hold true even for non-Shaker fans of this style that, according to Shaker belief, "That which has the highest use possesses the greatest beauty."

MODERN STYLES: BAUHAUS AND ART DECO

"Modern" is a slightly ambiguous term when it comes to classifying furniture styles. It basically encompasses all styles that have existed from about 1900 to the present, which is a wide range of styles difficult to categorize.

The Bauhaus School style (which was popular from about 1919 to 1933) incorporated minimalism and functionalism, and has had a serious effect on modern architecture and design. The Bauhaus School in Germany counted among its supporters physicist Albert Einstein and painter Marc Chagall.

Art Deco furniture became popular in the 1920s and 1930s, as did an entire Art Deco style of architecture and design, seen in many buildings in cities across the U.S., including the South Beach district of Miami and a wide assortment of buildings in Los Angeles. Characterized by streamlined, geometric forms, Art Deco furniture includes rounded fronts and wood mixed with chrome hardware, glass or other materials.

The photo above shows a classic example of the Art Deco style. This cabinet is made by Pollaro Custom Furniture, Inc. (www.pollaro.com).

measuring devices

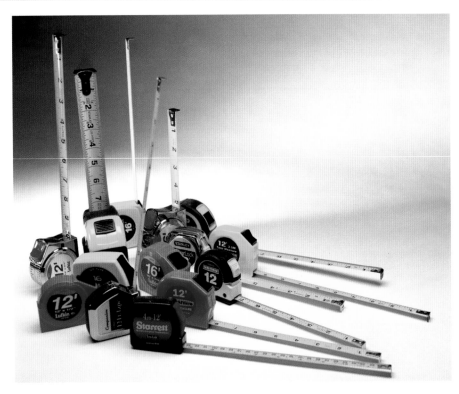

MEASURING DEVICES

- TAPE MEASURE: used for quick measures and measuring accurate lengths

- 3' STRAIGHTEDGE: used for drawing straight lines and accurate measuring

- 90° ANGLE DEVICE: used for measuring accurate angles

- ANGLE GAUGE: used for measuring angles and gauging angles

- COMPASS: used to divide lines and measure circles and arcs; also used to measure to create polygons

- PROTRACTOR: used for measuring angles and lines

- CARPENTER'S SQUARE: used as an adjustable slide for accurate measures across, at 45° angles and at 90° angles

- SPEED SQUARE (6" AND 12"): used for accurate straight lines, as well as rafter cuts and layouts

- T-SQUARE: used for larger square layouts

- FRENCH CURVE: used for laying out intricate designs for "fancier" projects

- OUTSIDE CALIPERS: used for measuring the thicknesses of items being turned on the lathe

Of course, every woodworker has a good tape measure, probably even two or three of them. Even most nonwoodworkers own at least one tape measure. It's probably the most utilized device in or out of the workshop.

It's good for measuring long boards without hauling a straightedge around or a folding tape. All measuring tapes are compact, except for those 100' tape measures, and even those are fairly small.

Most tape measures advance in increments of either $\frac{1}{16}$" or $\frac{1}{32}$".

The standard 1' ruler, yardstick or 3' straightedge are other items you will likely get a lot of use out of in your shop. All of the above can be used for measuring and/or drawing straight lines.

The most versatile and essential measuring devices are the 25' or 30' measuring tapes, the 6" and 12" speed square, and the movable-angle gauge, which is an incredibly versatile tool that allows you to precisely find the exact angle you need to make an odd angle.

Another unique tool is the center square, which can be used to find the center on a round object. Simply place it on the end of the dowel and line it up to the two pins underneath, make a cross hash each way, and there you go, there's the center.

Outside calipers are used most of the time for measuring thicknesses of items that are being turned on the lathe. They also seem to work excellently for spindle replacement on new furniture; you can use them to measure the peg that will go into the seat or the backrest.

standard guidelines for furniture

When designing your own furniture, the style and method options are endless. You may know that you like Arts & Crafts furniture, for example, and decide to implement certain characteristics from that style into your own designs. Or maybe you just see something you like in a magazine and want to try to make your own at home, rather than buying it from Ethan Allen or Art Van.

Whichever way you go, you're going to have to sketch out what you want before you do anything else, then make a pattern to follow.

A pattern is the full-size outline of the object that you are going to make, drawn on paper or a template board. Even furniture with unique curves and fancy outlines can be accomplished with a little bit of technique.

For patterns that you want to transfer from magazines or other photographs, you can do this through the use of large squares drawn on a sheet of paper. Draw the corresponding lines through the large squares in the same way they go through the small squares (on the original). After this is done, the pattern can be transferred to the template or master pattern by tracing it on carbon paper over the template. Be sure your pattern is secure to eliminate shifting or slippage.

One woodworker makes a lot of antler plaques, and although plaques are not necessarily in the furniture category, they provide a simple illustration of how half-patterns can be used. You can just cut a half-pattern of the plaque, then create a mirror image in wood. This can often apply to many furniture projects, as well.

Most patterns can be cut out with a band saw, jigsaw or coping saw. Band saws seem to work best, if you have one, because they make it easy to cut out the project's more minute details.

The Sheraton style of furniture provides an example of a rounded-leg curved pattern you might come across or use. The legs can be stacked together and cut

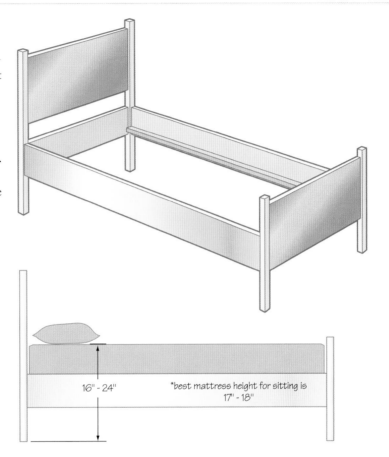

16" - 24"   *best mattress height for sitting is 17" - 18"

20" - 24"

36" - 40"

28" - 30"

in multiples of two or four, depending on your saw and its size. The final template should be sanded smooth for quality in your duplications. This would be your final pattern for that part of the project, so it should be as exact as possible.

One thing to note when cutting your pattern: Keep the blade on the outside of the line of the pattern, since you can always sand it or file it down, or saw some off, if you have to — but you can't add on to it!

It's also a good idea to use a $^1/_4$" underlay with your template. It can be readily cut on a band saw (or jigsaw) and can be sanded quickly or recut for final dimensioning. The templates are easy to store for later use if the need arises.

standard guidelines for shelving

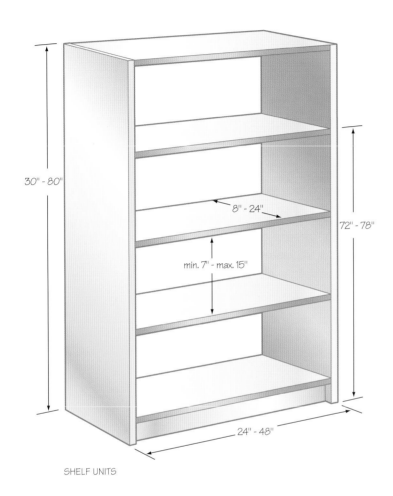

30" - 80"

8" - 24"

min. 7" - max. 15"

72" - 78"

24" - 48"

SHELF UNITS

A NOTE ON FURNITURE CONSTRUCTION AND PROJECT SIZE

One thing to keep in mind when constructing furniture of any sort in your workshop or basement (especially your basement) is size.

Don't learn the hard way that you have to be able to get your final project up the stairs and through the shop doorway.

Most woodworkers know at least one other woodworker who has done this: spent months perfecting a hutch or cabinet or dresser, only to realize upon completion that it won't fit through the shop door.

One woodworker has a horror story of building a snowmobile sled in his basement. The shop's 32" door simply would not allow the completed sled to exit. He had to remove the windshield to get it out.

Try to always put a 36" door in any workshop, or even larger if space allows. If you have the luxury or the forethought, create a workshop space ideal for cutting long boards and allowing for the mobility of large objects. A 32' x 16' shop would be ideal for ample maneuvering space, although most shops can be created smaller than that if you use your space efficiently.

SOME JOINT CHOICES FOR SHELF CONSTRUCTION

▪ BUTT JOINT: easy joint; use glue and nails

▪ CLEAT: simple joint; unsightly but economical

▪ FULL DADO: simple joint; fairly strong, but needs facing

▪ BLIND DADO: fairly intricate joint; very strong

▪ SLIDING DOVETAIL: strong and exact joint

▪ BISCUIT: simple joint; need to own the biscuit joiner tool; good for general shelf use

Shelves can vary in size from a 1' wall mount to 60" to 78" of floor shelves.

Keep in mind the reasons you have and the aesthetics you desire in building, for example, a bookcase. Particleboard might not be the best material in terms of sag and durability. Although particleboard is laminated on both sides and pretty thick, the weight can add up quickly. Hardwood seems to be the best choice for avoiding sag when building shelves.

Bookshelves are fairly uniform in size (for example, often 12" high and 11¹⁄₂" deep), but you can vary size to accommodate individual needs. If your length is going to exceed 36", it's a good idea to use a horizontal cleat for added strength. The back can be made out of lighter material, but it's also a good idea to rabbet your backboards for a square, flush fit. If you plan to use shelves for heavier books or objects, use a heavier plywood for the back and rabbet the backboard to keep the shelves snug and to avoid the possibility of sag.

Whether you're building shelves that will be used to hold CDs, magazines, photo albums or clothes, first measure the depth, height and width you plan to place the shelf unit in, thinking all the while about the décor of the rest of the room or unit.

RECONSTRUCTING A CHURCH PEW

One woodworker, Bernard Datema of Carson City, Michigan, came across an interesting find several years ago, which led to an interesting design solution. This is his tale:

I acquired an old church pew that was 8' long. To make two shorter seats from it, I measured to the center with a 2' square, squared it and cut it into two sections with a shill saw.

The seat ends were 2" thick, and the seat and back were inset into the dadoed ends 1" and secured with oak wedges and nails. Two new ends had been made of oak to match the existing wood. These new ends had to be notched in 1" to accept the other pew.

Here, I made a ¼" luan template to mortise my seat sides. Using the existing half of the old seat, I sat it on the end of the template and traced the outline of the seat and back. After I traced the outline, I cut out the narrow center with a jigsaw and sanded the edges.

The next step was to fasten it to the new pew ends with small brads. Then I used my router with a dovetail bit to make a continuous mortise for the entire seat. The shaft on the dovetail bit rode against the template and followed the pattern quite precisely.

Securing the seat to the ends was quite simple, with wedges driven in from the back and underneath and secured with screws at an angle.

The final step was installing a thick oak moulding on the back and underneath to cover the screws, wedges and gaps. The wedges drove the seat tightly to the visible part of the front.

What you're building becomes a piece of furniture once it's sitting in view, so take a few minutes to think about how you plan to give it some visual appeal, and not just the practical aspects.

If the sides and shelves are made of a high-quality wood, then you'll want to make the face from a top-quality wood, also. This will conceal any exposed edges to give your final project a finished look. Cleats attached to the front can also be appealing to the eye, if done in a smooth manner with detailed design. Feel free to use screws for greater strength anywhere they can be installed and not exposed to view.

COMMON SIZES OF SHELF-STORAGE OBJECTS

When building bookcases, entertainment units or any piece of furniture that is meant to hold things, use these handy dimensions to figure out the needed space for these common items.

	OBJECT	DEPTH × HEIGHT (INCHES)
Books	Paperback	$4^{1}/_{4} \times 6^{7}/_{8}$
	Standard hardback	$7 \times 9^{1}/_{2}$
	Large book (e.g., textbook)	9×11
	Art/coffee table book	11×15
Music	Vinyl LP	$12^{3}/_{8} \times 12^{3}/_{8}$
	Compact disc	$5^{1}/_{2} \times 5$
	Audiocassette	$2^{3}/_{4} \times 4^{1}/_{4}$
Video	Laser disc	$12^{3}/_{8} \times 12^{3}/_{8}$
	DVD	$5^{1}/_{2} \times 7^{1}/_{2}$
	VHS videocassette	$4^{1}/_{8} \times 7^{1}/_{2}$
	8mm VHS	$4^{1}/_{8} \times 7^{1}/_{2}$
Computer	CD-ROM	$5^{1}/_{2} \times 5$
	$3^{1}/_{2}$" floppy disk	$3^{1}/_{2} \times 3^{1}/_{2}$
	$5^{1}/_{4}$" floppy disk	$5^{1}/_{4} \times 5^{1}/_{4}$

standard guidelines for tables and chairs

Most tables, whether dining or card, are constructed to accommodate the average-size person in this so-to-speak average-size world designed for adults.

The most common table height is 29", but, as the sizes of humans vary, as well as the purposes of tables, that 29" number varies, as well.

Tables basically vary in height from 26" to 32". Drafting tables and kitchen bar tables are higher, which means the stools designed to accompany them are higher, as well.

If you are constructing a new card table or a new dining table for a particular home or family, take into consideration the general height of its members, and make the table and chairs taller or shorter for comfort.

The general rule is to allow 12" for a person's knees and 6" to 9" for leg clearance for each person sitting at the table. Try to allow at least 24" to 26" for each individual. Think about the last wedding reception you went to: They always seem to crowd a lot of uncomfortable guests at rectangular tables, but people sitting at crowded round tables don't seem as uncomfortable. Round tables seem to provide a little more room for each person.

When thinking about the chairs that will accompany a table, be aware that the taller the chair back, the more formal the chair appears. Also, more room is needed for formal tables, as chairs are often wider and may have armrests. For those situations, plan for at least 2" extra on each side.

The circumference of a round table can be calculated by multiplying the number of persons seated by 24" or 26", depending on style and chairs. Calculate the diameter by dividing the circumference by pi (3.14), and there you have it. If you've ever built something like a pole barn and thought to yourself, "I wish I would've made it a little larger," well ... apply that thought to table construction, as well!

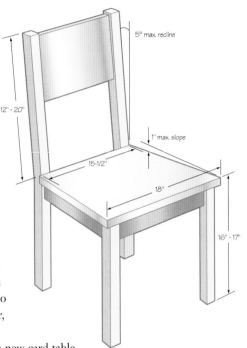

AVERAGE TABLE SIZES (IN INCHES)

TABLE TYPE	LENGTH	HEIGHT	WIDTH
Square card	32–40	28–30	32–40
Round card	48–50 dia.	28–32	
Dining	60–96	28–30	40–42
Oval dining	42–56	28–30	40–42
Workbench	36–?	32–36	24–28
Sofa table	48–72	24–30	16–20
Coffee	2/3 length of sofa	16–18	36–56
Oval coffee	2/3 length of sofa	16–18	30–36
Library	48–72	28–32	28–36
Entry hall	40–72	32–36	16–24
End	22–30	16–24	16–24
Nightstand	16–24	16–26	16–24
Drafting	36–60	28–40	24–40

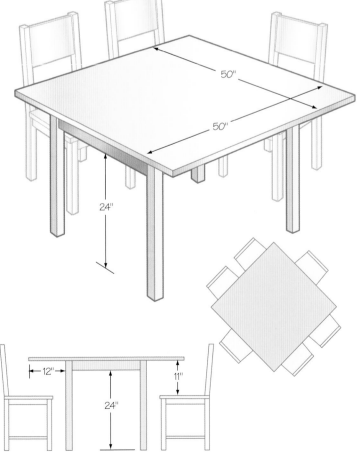

door and drawer construction

Drawers can be made in a number of different ways. The simplest way is the rabbet cut. Most rabbet-cut drawers are secured with nails and glue. A slot is cut in the bottom to accept the drawer bottom. Most people advise against gluing the bottom in because of wood expansion and contraction.

Another method of construction is the rabbet-and-tongue joint. This joint can also be nailed and glued, but it's a stronger joint. It's a bit more involved than a plain-cut rabbet joint. When a drawer needs to be repaired, it's often due to the drawer either being overloaded or underconstructed, and often a little of both. In almost every case, the sides of a drawer that needs to be repaired had been made of material that was too thin for its purpose, so that even dovetails end up broken and cracked. If you feel triangle wedges need to be installed while creating a drawer, then by all means do so on large, wide drawers. On larger drawers, if you have room, install a center brace from the front to the back underneath the drawer, for added stability.

The dovetail joint is a popular joint. It's also a very strong joint if it's made with the right quality materials. Most dovetail joints can be glued and clamped. They can be cut by hand or with a dovetail jig. The face of the drawer can be dovetailed or fastened to the front of the already-dovetailed front using screws and glue.

Drawer slides, rails or guides should be made of hardwood simply because of the wear they will receive. More modern metal roller slides are durable, are maintenance-free and have a catch that prevents the drawer from being pulled all the way open. Side-mount or bottom-mounted slides can be purchased at any home-improvement store. Bottom-mounted metal slides function most efficiently.

Most older drawer slides can be duplicated for repair because of their simple construction. Also, on a lot of older furniture, the side of the drawer often acts as a rail or an inner guide.

Probably one of the most common ways of making doors is the stile-and-rail method. These doors can be made with a shaper. Different styles of design allow for some very appealing looks. Never glue in a wood panel that goes into the stile-and-rail door because of wood expansion.

All of your panels must be free-floating. Doors can be overlapping (on the outside) or they can be set in the facing or framework.

COPE & STICK   SLIDING DOOR

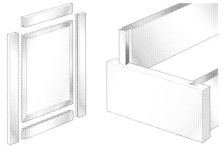

FRAME & PANEL   SLIDING DOVETAIL

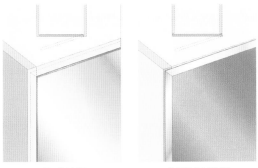

INSET DOOR   OVERLAY DOOR

THE MIRACLE OF WAX ON WOOD

Waxing the rail of a drawer is a good way to prevent wear and allow for mobility. An old candle works great for this. Wax is an excellent lubricant for wood drawers.

One dramatic example of this involves the historic and unusual home of the author of this book. I live in a restored building that was once the reception hall next to St. John the Baptist Catholic Church in Hubbardston, Michigan, where many of my relatives had wedding receptions and other gatherings throughout the years. About 15 years ago, a neighbor of mine, Bud Datema, had the hall moved from its original location to his property about five miles away. Bud renovated this 30' by 70' building that I currently live in. But moving it five miles was no easy task. To get the building off its foundation and onto the I-beams for transport, the mover Bud hired used ¾" waxed hardwood slats.

The only sound you could hear as the giant historic building creeped down the lone country road was the creaking of the building itself as it was sliding on the I-beams.

Now that's several tons of wood, so you know wax will work well for a simple fix!

Another construction method is to biscuit joint at 45° angles. A simple method, it must be precise and square. It's quick and easy, but should be clamped as any glued joint should.

Half-lap joints are also quite simple, but again, care should be taken in making accurate cuts. The miter lock is another method and will definitely give you a tight joint. It involves several cuts.

The framework of a cupboard or cabinet can be jointed with biscuits, dowels or mortise-and-tenon joinery. Mortise-and-tenon joints will give the strongest, tightest fit. It's fairly labor-intensive, but well worth the effort. Biscuit joinery is, again, simple.

PROFILES OF TWO FURNITURE DESIGNERS: SAM MALOOF AND DAVID LYNCH

SAM MALOOF

The Renwick Gallery of the Smithsonian American Art Museum presented the first full-scale exhibition dedicated to the furniture of world-renowned woodworker Sam Maloof last year. *The Furniture of Sam Maloof* explored the craftsmanship, style, life and legacy of the designer-craftsman with 65 pieces of furniture ranging from rocking chairs to dining tables and music stands.

"The exhibition (was) a fascinating look at Maloof's unique style and the evolution of his exquisite furniture," said Elizabeth Broun, the museum's Margaret and Terry Stent Director.

Maloof is best known for his all-wood rocking chairs enjoyed by three former U.S. presidents. He became the first craft artist to receive a coveted MacArthur Foundation Fellowship, or "genius" grant, in 1985 and was honored with the American Craft Council's prestigious Gold Medal in 1988.

In honor of the exhibition, former president Jimmy Carter (a woodworker himself) wrote a letter to Maloof stating, "For more than 50 years, you have shared your art and woodworking skills with anyone who has had the good fortune to know you. Your friends have become your customers, and your customers have become friends. Your passion for life, and for your craft, is obvious in every piece of your exquisite furniture. You richly deserve even more acclaim than has been given you."

Jeremy Adamson, curator of the exhibition and former Renwick senior curator, said, "Maloof created a seamless 'craftsman lifestyle,' integrating his craft into all aspects of his life and considering himself a woodworker first, and a designer second. He built his unique, artistic home — now listed on the National Register of Historic Places — room by room over 40 years. Maloof's home, attached directly to his workshop, is filled with his own furniture and collections of art and crafts, providing a unique showroom for his functional forms."

Maloof has always had a consistent drive toward a single goal — the perfection of his original prototypes. He makes continual minor adjustments to these prototypes, resulting in sculptural furniture that is beautiful to look at and at the same time comfortable and functional.

Maloof was born in Chino, California, in 1916 to Lebanese immigrants. He received no formal training or experience in furniture making, but rather began as a commercial artist. His first major commission came in 1952 from industrial designer Henry Dreyfuss and led to the development of his sculptural style.

Maloof adopted unique techniques, such as a freehand use of the band saw, and invented signature features, such as the "hard" line and the dado-rabbet or Maloof joint. The "hard" line is a raised ridge running down the legs and arms of furniture pieces for aesthetic purposes, while the dado-rabbet joint is a remarkably strong joint that creates a cleaner line. At the age of 85, Maloof continues to employ these techniques during his daily work in his studio.

The exhibition was organized by the Renwick Gallery of the Smithsonian American Art Museum.

A virtual exhibition, which you can view at the museum's Web site (www.americanart.si.edu), combines images of Maloof's furniture along with quotations from the artist.

The Furniture of Sam Maloof, a book written by Adamson and copublished with W.W. Norton, is based on new information from the Maloof workshop papers and locates Maloof's work within the history of the American craft movement. The heavily illustrated publication features photography by Jonathan Pollock. Adamson is currently chief of the Prints and Photographs Division at the Library of Congress.

The Renwick Gallery of the Smithsonian American Art Museum is dedicated to exhibiting American crafts from the 19th to the 21st century. The Renwick is located on Pennsylvania Avenue at 17th Street N.W. in Washington, D.C.

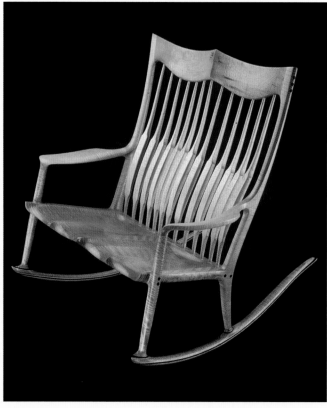

This is a double rocking chair designed by Sam Maloof.

PHOTO COURTESY OF THE RENWICK GALLERY

David Lynch, film director and furniture designer.

Photos above and below show David Lynch's unique table designs.

DAVID LYNCH

Yes, *the* David Lynch, the director of such avant-garde, and often puzzling, films as *Blue Velvet* and *Mulholland Dr.*

But a furniture designer?

"Films and furniture are based on ideas," Lynch has said, conceptually connecting his two hobbies. "You get an idea. And then you're hooked. And building is as important as designing, because many times design grows as one is building."

Lynch designs and builds the prototypes of his furniture creations in his shop in Hollywood. The company Casanostra in Switzerland (www.casanostra.com) has been manufacturing Lynch's designs and selling them under the series title "The City of Absurdity."

But by the end of this year, Casanostra will cease production, and the furniture of David Lynch will become part of the Veit Rausch Collection, which claims to be a company comprised of objects that complement people's daily lives and influence their thinking.

The collection avoids using the word "furniture," preferring the word "tools" to refer to these items that help people in their daily lives. With this concept in mind, a collection is being built up by taking works of universal-thinking artists.

Furniture designs include an asymmet-rical espresso table, a seemingly off-kilter one-legged steel block table, as well as a VCR case and a table that were used in the film *Lost Highway*, both designed by Lynch.

"To my mind, most tables are too big and they're too high," says Lynch on Casanostra's Web site. "They shrink the size of the room and eat into space and cause unpleasant mental activity."

Lynch, who says he "daydreams of furniture," has been designing furniture secretly for many years. He presented his furniture collection at the Salone del Mobile in Milan, Italy, in 1997.

Of woodworking and furniture making, Lynch says, "It's a special outlook. You build your own world. And, in my case, my father always had a workshop in the house, and I was taught how to use tools and spent a lot of time in the shop building things, so it all started at a young age."

CHAPTER **5**

> hand tools

planes, chisels and files

When you're out shopping for your shop, it's easy to get mesmerized by all of those high-falutin modern power tools. It's also easy to fall under the misconception that power tools are the only way to achieve woodworking perfection. Just look at the intricate, high-quality furnishings that were produced in the 17th, 18th and 19th centuries. Those craftsmen worked without a power tool to their name. And you can, too!

Just because hand tools aren't plugged into electric sockets doesn't mean they're safe. Be cautious; watch and learn from experienced woodworkers how to confidently and properly handle all of your woodworking tools. Never lose respect for the tools you're using and never forget that hand tools can be just as dangerous as power tools.

using your hands

HAND PLANES

Measuring and marking tools are the most logical subject when initiating a conversation about hand tools. From the rudimentary chalk line to the bevel gauge, quite a few hand tools are available to assist in the measuring and marking of your projects. But as these were discussed in chapter four, we will skip right to the fun stuff.

For some reason, hand planes are one of the most sensually pleasing woodworking tools to hold and to use. The shape of the tool, contoured to your hand, with a firm grip, makes you feel like you're in charge of your woodworking project while keeping you closely connected to it. You can feel and hear the wood beneath your hands as it peels off in (what you hope are) even, level strips. Handsaws are similar in this manner.

So what are hand planes used for? And what are your hand plane options?

In general, hand planes are used to smooth the surface of a piece of wood. The plane's body, made of metal or wood, holds a metal blade at a particular, fixed angle to the wood and is drawn across the wood in a scraping motion to "true up" the surface. Hand planes have depth adjustments on them to change the depth of the blade's cutting edge.

Shaping planes are a little more intricate, as they are used to shape contours. Hollow planes, in particular, can be used to hollow out things such as bowls.

You can buy some pretty fancy hand planes for up to hundreds of dollars from places like Lee Valley and Garrett Wade, but you also can't go wrong with an old Stanley hand plane that you inherited from your father or find at an antique store (after a little restoration work to remove the rust, of course).

The picture above shows a bench plane.

This is a shoulder plane.

HANDSAWS

First, know that handsaws are great exercise. The power comes from your own hand (hence, the name), rather than the electric power of a circular saw or a miter saw. When it comes to saws, you'll find that the fewer teeth per inch (TPI) on the blade, the faster and rougher the cut will be. More TPI means you'll get a slower but more precise cut.

Some handsaws are made for very particular tasks, such as cutting tight curves (coping saws) or cutting intricate dovetail joints (the gent's saw). But you'll most often come into contact with these basics: the crosscut saw, the ripsaw and the Japanese ryoba saw.

Crosscut saws are used for cuts that you want to make across the wood grain. Crosscut saws usually come with 8 to 12 TPI.

Ripsaws are used for cuts that you want to make with the wood grain. Your cut will be rougher than with a crosscut saw, as ripsaws have fewer TPI, usually from 5 to 7.

Above is a crosscut handsaw.

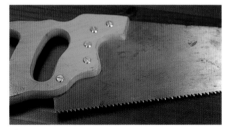

This is a ripping handsaw.

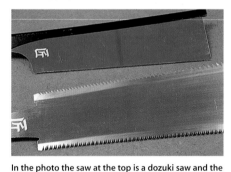

In the photo the saw at the top is a dozuki saw and the saw at the bottom is a ryoba saw.

Japanese saws work on the pull and have narrow kerfs. Kataba-nokogiri (noko-giri means saw) is a saw with teeth on one side; ryoba-nokogiri, a saw with teeth on both sides (one edge for ripping and the other for crosscutting), and dozuki-noko-giri is a saw with a stiffener.

Ryoba saws are used for general cutting purposes. The kugihiki saw is great for cutting things flush to the surface, such as cutting a dowel peg overhang flush to its surface. The dozuki is good for cutting dovetails and other types of joinery.

These clamps are, left to right: a deep-throat quick clamp, a spring clamp, a level-operated quick clamp, a one-hand operated quick clamp, another style of a one-hand operated quick clamp, a combination quick clamp with screw tightener, two styles of quick clamps with screw tighteners and a C-clamp.

SCRAPING AND SMOOTHING TOOLS

Scraping and smoothing hand tools are used by general woodworkers, but also are often utilized by specialty woodworkers, such as woodturners and woodcarvers. If you work in those two latter fields, you may have a much bigger arsenal of gouges and chisels than the average woodworker.

But if you're a novice, you want at least the following basics.

CHISELS

With big, thick blades, chisels are a necessity in any woodshop. Most obviously, they can be used to chunk out big pieces of wood from a cut. Chisels quickly shape and smooth wood when cutting mortises or other joints. At your local hardware or home-improvement store you'll see a wide variety of chisels in a wide variety of sizes, ranging approximately from $1/8$" to 2", and with mostly self-explanatory names, such as paring (or butt) chisels, framing chisels, mortising chisels and crank-neck chisels.

Gouges, which fall into the chisel family but have been modified to include a hollowed blade, are used for roughing out stock or gouging out hollows into wood surfaces.

RASPS, FILES AND SPOKESHAVES

Rasps are used for shaping wood wherever a chisel might be too large and clumsy or might create tear-out in your project. You'll find rasps in flat, half-round and round shapes and in a range of coarseness-es. Files are basically rasps but offer a finer cut. Spokeshaves, which must be pushed or

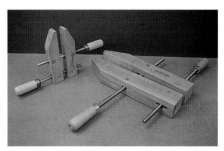

Hand screws are great for gluing angled joints because the jaws can be adjusted out of parallel.

pulled with both hands, are used for shaping and smoothing rounded objects, such as spokes or spindles.

CLAMPS

As every experienced woodworker knows, you can never have enough clamps.

Clamps do as their name implies: They clamp elements of an assembly together, either to hold the shape, hold secure to a worktable or hold pieces together in place during glue-up. Some of the most common clamps are:

C-clamps: These small, powerful clamps are useful for smaller projects.

Pipe clamps: These inexpensive clamps are versatile and simple.

Spring clamps: These quick, easy-to-use clamps are like giant clothespins; they're simple, but don't work for heavy situations.

Hand screws: These clamps, which have been around for ages, are made of project-friendly wood, have deep throats and can be adjusted to different angles.

Miter clamps: These clamps hold mitered frames or joints together.

The picture above shows a finely sharpened chisel.

On the left is a round or rat-tail rasp and on the right is a combination flat and curved rasp.

Gouges come in many sizes.

This is a homemade wooden mallet.

WOODWORKING HAS BEEN AROUND A LONG TIME

Microscopic wood particles on 1.5-million-year-old tools show woodworking is an old hobby

Spanish archaeologists have discovered the earliest evidence of woodworking.

There is a consensus among many anthropologists that early humans who lived in the African savannas between 2 million and 1.5 million years ago were mainly scavenging creatures who lacked the intelligence and technology to hunt animals. However, a recent discovery in the Peninj region in Tanzania demonstrates a much higher level of technological sophistication during this period than previously believed.

A team of Spanish archaeologists, led by Dr. Manuel Dominguez-Rodrigo, from the Complutense University of Madrid, found residues of wood on the working edges of stone hand axes found in the region. The stone tools also show clear damage due to having been used in heavy-duty activities. These important findings push the appearance of human woodworking back by 1 million years.

SEARCH

"This is the oldest evidence of woodworking in human evolution," said Dominguez-Rodrigo. "The remains belonging to acacia trees are proof that early humans had wooden utensils, such as spears and digging sticks, which very likely enabled them to have the technology necessary to become successful hunters."

Other team members involved in the discovery include Prof. Jordi Juan-Treserres, a paleobotanist from the University of Barcelona; Prof. Jordi Serrallonga, an archaeologist from the University of Barcelona; Dr. Luis Alcala, paleontologist and vice-director of the Natural History Museum in Madrid, and Dr. Luis Luque, geologist from the Natural History Museum. The project has been funded through the Spanish Ministry of Culture, the Complutense University, and Earthwatch Institute.

The emergence of complex stone tools around 1.5 million years ago, with the so-called Acheulian technology, shows that early humans were endowed with a sophisticated dexterity in crafting some tools. However, these large bifacial artifacts, among which hand axes are the most common, were inefficient hunting weapons. Archaeological remains in early sites show that these early humans used the stone tools to butcher animals. For most archaeologists the lack of other artifacts suggests the lack of the adequate technology for a hunting way of life, until now.

The area of Peninj contains some of the oldest archaeological sites in the world with Acheulian tools. Most of the fossil fauna discovered by the Spanish team belong to animals that suggest a very open and dry savanna environment. Equids (like modern zebras), antilopini (like modern gazelles) and alcelaphini (like modern wildebeests) constitute most of the animals discovered. The fossil pollen discovered also indicates a very open landscape dominated by grasslands and a smaller number of trees among which acacia is the best represented. Some plant residues discovered (called phytoliths) show that the type of grass most represented is a short grass that grows in very open and dry ecosystems.

Peninj exhibits the most open paleolandscape of all the areas where archaeological sites dated to 2 million to 1.5 million years have been discovered so far. This means that the availability of vegetable resources must have been very limited for early humans here. It also means that the availability of scavengeable resources must have been fairly small, since open landscapes are always full with competing carnivores.

Dominguez-Rodrigo suggests that Peninj provides a unique scenario to test some of the most relevant hypotheses on human evolution. His team is attempting to answer questions such as: How did early humans survive in such a harsh environment? Did they hunt or did they scavenge for survival? If these hominids hunted, making them the earliest hunters in human history, what did their technology consists of? By studying the technology of these early humans, the team hopes to get a glimpse on how intelligent they were.

Ongoing studies in Peninj show that strong competition of carnivores in the area must have prevented early humans from obtaining animal protein resources through scavenging. On the contrary, the analyses of bones from the archaeological sites show that hominids were exploiting fully fleshed animal carcasses. This is indicated by the amount of cut marks made with stone tools on anatomical sections where flesh is nonexistent if carnivores had consumed the animals before hominids did. This fact suggest that early humans

An example of a primitive woodworking tool.

IMAGE COURTESY OF EARTHWATCH INSTITUTE

IMAGE COURTESY OF EARTHWATCH INSTITUTE

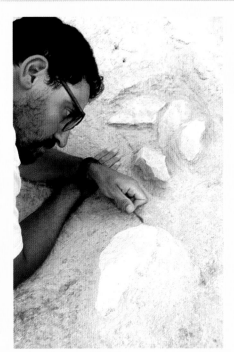

IMAGE COURTESY OF EARTHWATCH INSTITUTE

relevant for the study of human evolution: Humans were involved in woodworking activities more than a million years before the oldest evidence that we had until now. Early humans, at a very early stage of their evolution, were producing wooden implements that have not been preserved in the archaeological record. According to this discovery, rudimentary spears could have been one type of wooden artifact that humans were making 1.5 million years ago. This could have enhanced their adaptation as hunters to open environments, and gives us a further insight into the complex intelligence of hominids at that time.

"The discovery of early woodworking technology shows that human intelligence at its beginnings was far more complex than accepted so far," said Dominguez-Rodrigo. "It also shows that early humans were active agents in the modification of the environment, instead of passive animals like the rest of the fauna as they were pictured until now."

Earthwatch volunteers working with Dr. Dominguez-Rodrigo last year helped expand on the team's findings in Peninj, further refining the analysis of this important find. Earthwatch Institute is an international nonprofit organization that supports scientific field research worldwide by offering members of the public unique opportunities to work alongside leading field scientists and researchers. The Institute's mission is to promote sustainable conservation of our natural resources and cultural heritage by creating partnerships between scientists, educators and the general public.

Thanks to the Earthwatch Institute (www.earthwatch.org) for this story.

were hunting these animals unearthed at Peninj. Dominguez-Rodrigo's team is attempting to find out how.

One of the archaeological sites in Peninj has provided the team with a critical part of the answer. An assemblage of over 200 stone tools has been excavated in a nicely preserved context. This has allowed for the first time the discovery of well-preserved microscopic remains on the edges of the tools caused by their use 1.5 million years ago. The team has carefully analyzed the artifacts and the surrounding soil for plant residues. Plant residues belonging to grasses have been found in the soil, but the residues found on the artifacts are different. They appear only on the surface of the edges of the hand axes, which are worn by hard use. The microscopic plant remains found on the hand axes have been identified as belonging to acacia trees, indicating that the hominids were chopping wood.

The meaning of this discovery is very

CHAPTER **6**

> power tools
saws, routers, sanders and more

Woodworkers and their power tools. It's almost not necessary to outline what types of power tools are on the market, as most novice woodworkers have an intimate relationship with the tool aisle at the local home-improvement center before they even attempt their first project. To many woodworkers, it's all about the tools (insert Tim Allen grunting noise here).

In fact, there is a special day set aside for tools: March 11 is — and this is a fact — Worship of Tools Day. Of course, this celebration exists in the hearts of many craftsmen 365 days a year.

While the old-fashioned and stubborn may insist that you can build anything with hand tools that you can build with power tools, it's definitely true that power tools save a lot of time and a lot of sore muscles.

But you need to acquaint yourself with what's out there and what your woodworking needs will be before you go out and spend a fortune on very nice, but possibly very frivolous, power tools.

what's out there

It's unarguable that power tools make a woodworker's life easier. They also make it more expensive — unless you consider time to be money, because power tools definitely save the former.

The kind of woodworking you'll be doing dictates which tools you absolutely must have in your shop. A great overview of all the tools you might need is *The Insider's Guide to Buying Tools* (Popular Woodworking, 2000); it discusses in detail the uses, pros and cons of everything from air tools to biscuit joiners.

If you're going to be making furniture, you almost have to have a table saw. Which, of course, means you almost have to have a dust collector. From there, it becomes more individualized. Power tools are available in two general categories: portable and stationary (also called "floor models"). There are miter saws, drill presses, jigsaws, jointers, planers, routers, scroll saws and more. And, if you plan to do your own spindle turning or other turning, you'll need a lathe.

But first things first.

TABLE SAWS

According to *The Insider's Guide to Buying Tools*, the table saw is the single most im-portant tool in your woodworking shop. It's true . . . the table saw, if you have one, is definitely the centerpiece around which the rest of your shop revolves. Unless you're going to be crosscutting and ripping all of your wood with a circular saw, you won't go far without a table saw.

Table saws are used not only for ripping and crosscutting, but for making joints by cutting dadoes, tenons and other elements, all at a variety of angles.

And table saws are only as good as the blades in them; sharp, clean blades are essential. You'll need different blades for different tasks. For example, ripping blades, which have generally large teeth and the fewest teeth per inch (TPI), are used (obviously) for ripping, and crosscutting blades, which crosscut solid-wood stock, have smaller teeth and about 60 TPI. Dado blades are used for cutting grooves wider than a regular single blade can cut.

BAND SAWS

Band saws are available in both portable and stationary models. They're most commonly used for following template curves or for cutting wood into usable sizes. What makes the band saw unique is its continuous, flexible, steel blade, which comes in a variety of widths and tooth grinds.

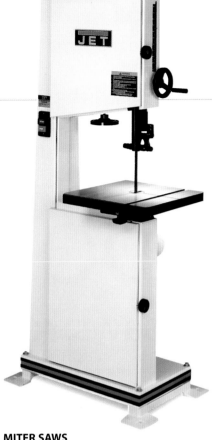

MITER SAWS

Typically, miter saws are used for cutting angles. Your choices include conventional miter saws, compound miter saws (which allow for more complex cuts) and sliding compound miter saws (which offer the most intricate crosscut capabilities). The conventional miter saws basically cut 45° angles, while the more complex and more expensive compound miter saws cut a variety of angles. Pay attention to the types of blades available; they can be specific to the type of cut you desire in a particular task or project.

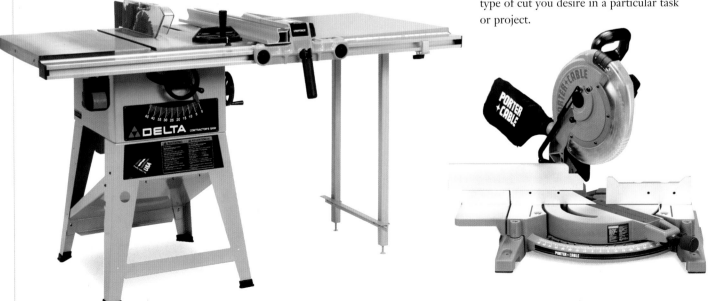

JIGSAWS

Jigsaws are handy little tools that come in both corded and cordless forms. They're kind of the portable version of the band saw. What they lack in power, jigsaws make up for in versatility. They can cut through wood, metal and plastic, depending on the type of blade you have inserted. Jigsaws are great for cutting circles or curves.

DRILLS

Drills are essential tools that have infinite uses even outside of the woodshop. Like other portable tools, they come in corded or cordless varieties. Drills are mostly used for drilling holes or attaching fasteners. Like routers, drills come with a wide range of accessories, such as jigs, drill guides and drill bits. Although drills come in different sizes, the $\frac{3}{8}$"drill is the most common in woodshops.

ROUTERS

So many options and uses are available for routers that entire books have been written about this versatile tool. There are standard (or "fixed-base") routers and plunge routers. They can be used to create mouldings, mortises and wide grooves. You can choose from a vast array of router accessories, depending on your needs. These include an infinite variety of router bit attachments, foot switches, jigs, speed controls, template guides and more.

BISCUIT JOINERS

To some, the biscuit joiner is a magical tool that allows quick assemblies of projects and strong joints. The joiner tool itself basically just drills biscuit slots into a joint corner into which a wooden biscuit (after being dipped in glue) is inserted, forming the joint attachment. More and more (once skeptical) woodworkers are being won over by the ease and simplicity of the biscuit joiner. In fact, an entire book of biscuit joiner projects is available through Popular Woodworking Books — *The Biscuit Joiner Project Book* by Jim Stack.

DRILL PRESSES

Portable (or benchtop) as well as stationary drill presses are available. Used for drilling holes at specific angles and depths, drill presses come in a wide variety of sizes. Different drill bit attachments are available, such as Forstner bits (which cut very neat, flat-bottomed holes and also can be used to enlarge existing holes) and plug cutter bits (which cut tenons or up to 1"-diameter plugs for covering counter-bored screws).

JOINTERS AND PLANERS

Jointers and planers come in both benchtop and stationary models. The individual stationary models are large, expensive machines that take up quite a bit of shop space; if space is an issue for you, combination jointer/planer models are available, as well. Basically, planers use metal cutters to smooth out your rough-sawn lumber, making both sides of a board parallel. Jointers offer a continuation of this board-preparation process and take the place of the sweaty exercise involved in hand-planing smooth the faces and edges of boards.

LATHES

Lathes also come in portable and stationary models. If you'd rather not take the easy way out and buy preturned legs and spindles, then you'll need at least a small benchtop lathe. Bigger, stationary lathes are often in the realm of serious furniture makers and of woodworkers who focus mostly on decorative turning, creating delicate wood pieces such as vases and bowls. Basically, a lathe supports a blank of wood and turns it, then the woodworker uses a tool such as a gouge against the quickly spinning wood to create the desired size and shape.

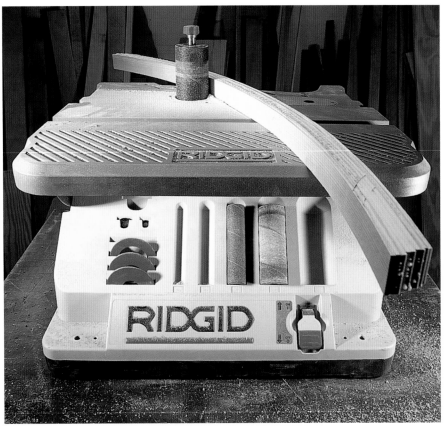

CIRCULAR SAWS

A circular saw is one of the most flexible hand power tools available. This saw can be used to crosscut, rip, cut angles by tilting the base, cut dadoes, make plunge cuts (for making cutouts for sinks in countertops, for example) and more. An entire house could be constructed using this tool as your only saw. Different blades are available depending on what materials you need to cut.

The more expensive saws have a worm drive connecting the motor to the blade rather than the traditional direct drive. The worm drive has proven itself to be effective in promoting motor life. It is recommended that a heavy-duty extension cord be used with these saws as they have high amperage ratings.

SANDERS

The wide variety of sanders includes random-orbit, belt, oscillating-spindle, stationary and more. Each sander has a different application. Stationary sanders, such as belt/disc sanders, are so powerful that they not only sand wood smooth, they can flatten and square it. Portable hand-held sanders are more common in the individual woodshop. They're used to shape and smooth project surfaces and edges.

DUST COLLECTION

Dust collection is about your own health and about shop cleanliness. You'll never escape the fact that woodworking produces wood dust. But with a good dust collection system in place, you can reduce your risks of lung or breathing problems. Each tool needs its own system attached, but you can also invest in simple wet/dry vacuum or an air cleaner.

VICTORIA AND ALBERT MUSEUM IN LONDON

The collection of more than 14,000 pieces from Great Britain, Europe and America is mostly furniture

If you're ever in London and you're a woodworker, stop at the world's greatest museum of design and the arts. Almost 700 people work at the Victoria and Albert Museum in London, England, with specialties ranging from conservation to design.

The museum's collection, which is predominantly of furniture, consists of more than 14,000 pieces from Great Britain, Europe and America, dating from the Middle Ages to the present day.

Besides furniture, the collection also includes related objects such as architectural and decorative woodwork, musical instruments, leatherwork, treen and clocks. You'll also find at the museum complete rooms, some of which are on display in the newly refurbished British Galleries, while the office designed for Edgar J. Kaufmann Jr. can be seen in the Frank Lloyd Wright Gallery.

The collections span 2,000 years of art in almost every medium, from many parts of the world. If you visit, you'll be stunned by the vast array of amazing and beautiful objects.

The museum was established in 1852, following the incredible success of the Great Exhibition the year before. The main goal of the exhibition was to make works of art available to all, to educate working people and to inspire British designers and manufacturers. Profits from the exhibition were used to establish the Museum of Manufactures, as it was initially known.

The museum moved to its present site in 1857 and was renamed the South Kensington Museum. Its collections expanded rapidly as it acquired the best examples of metalwork, furniture, textiles and all other forms of decorative art from all periods.

It also acquired fine art, such as paintings, drawings, prints and sculpture, in order to tell a more complete history of art and design.

Generous funding and a less competitive art market than today's allowed the young museum to make many important acquisitions.

The northern front of what is now the Pirelli Garden was the result of an ambitious extension plan in the 1860s and formed the main entrance to the museum at that time.

The museum itself also grew, with new buildings being added as and when needed. Many of these buildings, with their iron frames and glass roofs, were intended to be semipermanent exhibition halls, but they have all survived and are one of the finest groups of Victorian buildings in Great Britain.

In 1899, Queen Victoria laid the foundation stone of a new building designed to give the museum a grand facade and main entrance. To mark the occasion, it was renamed the Victoria and Albert Museum, in memory of the enthusiastic support Prince Albert had given to its foundation.

Throughout the 20th century, the collections continued to grow. While expanding its historical collections, the Victoria and Albert also maintained its acquisition of contemporary objects, starting with a collection of Art Nouveau furniture in 1900.

The museum's ceramics, glass, textiles, dress, silver, ironwork, jewelry, furniture, sculpture, paintings, prints and photographs now span the cultures of Europe, North America, Asia and North Africa, and date from ancient times to the present day.

Although the museum's collections are international in scope, they contain many particularly important British works, particularly British silver, ceramics, textiles and furniture. The British collections enable the Victoria and Albert to explain not just the history of design in the British Isles but also the broader sweep of their cultural history. The British Galleries are designed to give visitors from Great Britain and from around the world a new insight into the history of Great Britain by bringing visitors closer to the thoughts and lives of key people in an influential culture.

The Victoria and Albert Museum also offers visitors the chance to experience firsthand the splendor of the arts of Asia. Britain's long association with India and Southeast Asia has given the museum the opportunity to acquire magnificent works from the cultures of that region. Objects in all media are represented, including stone and bronze sculpture, furniture and woodwork, jewelry, metalwork and collections of Indian miniature painting and textiles that are among the most important in the world.

Contemporary design has always been at the heart of the Victoria and Albert's work, and the museum remains true to its founding mission of promoting excellence in design and manufacturing. It works hard to encourage contemporary designers, acquiring their work, and providing inspiration through its displays.

VICTORIA AND ALBERT MUSEUM

Cromwell Road
South Kensington
London SW7 2RL
www.vam.ac.uk

CHAPTER **7**

glues and adhesives

what to use

Webster's defines *glues* and *adhesives* as basically the same things, but according to Ernest Joyce's *Encyclopedia of Furniture Making*, traditional practice prefers *glue* when referring to bonding paper and wood, and *adhesive* when referring to bonding all other materials. At any rate, glues, particularly those made from animals, have been in use for thousands of years.

If you've been an Elmer's user your whole life, you might not realize the wide variety of glues that are out there on the market. Types range from all-purpose yellow glues to contact cement to epoxy glues to polyurethane glues. Each has its own adhesive specialty, and each has its own advantages and disadvantages.

making it stick

ADHESIVES DEFINED

The glues of yore, the simple hide glues and yellow glues that most woodworkers used well into the last century and still use today, have the advantages of being simple to understand and simple to use. Their main disadvantage, of course, has been their inability to resist moisture. Today, the many alternatives to the traditional glues address a variety of woodworking needs, but are very scientific in nature, can be toxic and dangerous, and can be a bit complicated for the novice to understand.

Besides the obvious function of holding two pieces of wood together, adhesives also perform the function of transferring and distributing stress of a formed unit, which increases a constructed unit's strength and firmness.

Adhesives generally fall into three basic categories: animal glues, vegetable glues and synthetic resin glues.

Animal glues are made from collagen, the primary protein that comes from an animal's skin, bone or muscle, mixed with hot water. Animal glues can also be made from the serum albumin that comes from either fresh blood or a dried-blood powder; these are mostly used in the creation of plywood.

Vegetable glues are often made from the starch and dextrin found in corn, wheat, potatoes or rice. Gum extracted from trees can also be used as an adhesive.

Synthetic glues are man-made polymers that can be changed or modified to meet particular woodworking needs. They have incredible water resistance and are divided into two basic categories: thermosetting adhesives and thermoplastic adhesives.

Thermosetting adhesives are activated via a condensation reaction in which water is eliminated, putting the adhesive through an irreversible chemical and physical change that makes it insoluble. Chemicals, heat or both act as the catalyst to force this change. Thermosetting adhesives include urea-formaldehyde, melamine formalde-

hyde, phenol formaldehyde and resorcinol formaldehyde.

Thermoplastic adhesives are prepolymerized and do not go through a chemical linking reaction as they cure, which means they remain in a reversible state and can be softened by heating. Thermoplastic adhesives include white glues (polyvinyl acetate emulsions) and hot-melt glues.

You can categorize your glue choices in other ways, besides grouping them under the animal, vegetable and synthetic headings.

Nick Engler, in his book *Nick Engler's Woodworking Wisdom* (Rodale Press, 1997), categorizes glues a bit differently, dividing them into four main groups: one-part glues that typically come ready to use in an applicator; two-part glues that come as a resin and a hardener and must be mixed before use; elastomers that remain flexible even after curing; and thermoplastic glues that change from solid to liquid when heated.

ANIMAL AND VEGETABLE GLUES
Animal Protein Glues

Animal protein glues, which include hide glues, come in both solid and liquid forms. Solid forms must be added to water, melted and kept warm during use and, in the end, have low resistance to moisture. These glues are sometimes used in the assembly of general furniture projects, but mostly work well for constructing stringed instruments and repairing antique furniture. Hide glue, specifically, is inexpensive and dries clear, is fairly useful for filling in gaps and is nontoxic, but has its downfall in the fact that it's not waterproof.

Blood Protein Glues

Blood protein glues are solid and are mixed with water and chemicals such as lime or caustic soda and have a little more resistance to moisture than animal protein glues. They're generally used for interior-use softwood plywoods, but have been replaced in the woodworking world with phenolic adhesives.

ADHESIVES COME IN MANY FORMS

Knowledge and use of adhesives is not new. The ancient Egyptians knew well the art of veneering and used adhesives to attach decorations to wood some 3,500 years before Christ.

Mud, dung and clay, along with mixtures of these substances, must also be regarded as adhesives and have been used for centuries to build huts in many parts of the world. Thatched huts plastered with a mixture of camel's dung and mud are still regularly used in southwestern Saudi Arabia, for example.

Many types of glue have been used to bond wood together, but until the time of the Second World War, essentially all of the glues were of natural origin. Adhesives based on synthetic polymers were introduced just before WWII and now surpass most of the older natural glues in importance for wood bonding.

These synthetic adhesives are used in situations that are far too demanding for adhesives of natural origin and satisfy moisture, durability and strength requirements that were unthinkable a few years ago. At one time, adhesives belonged exclusively in the realm of craftsmen; today, they have become indispensable to the engineer, as well.

–extracted from Brief Survey of Wood Adhesives *by Carl A. Eckelman, Forestry and Natural Resources, Purdue University Cooperative Extension Service, West Lafayette, Indiana*

SYNTHETIC GLUES
White and Yellow Glues

The most common and popular glues are white and yellow glues.

White glues, known scientifically as polyvinyl acetate, are commonly used for general woodworking, model-making projects and making repairs that involve porous materials such as paper or leather. White glues give a colorless bond line and are applied in liquid form directly to the wood and must be pressed at room tem-

WOOD SPECIES' EASE OF BONDING

It helps to understand that, regardless of the type of glue or adhesive you use, certain wood species bond more easily than others.

Before you begin a project, be aware that Osage orange and persimmon, which are hardwoods, do not bond easily. The imported woods rosewood and teak also bond with great difficulty.

Hardwoods that bond fairly well, but with some minor difficulty include: white ash, beech, birch, cherry, hickory, madrona, hard maple, and red and white oak, as well as the imported bubinga species. Softwoods that bond fairly well include yellow cedar and southern pine.

Hardwoods that bond well include butternut, elm, soft maple, sycamore, tupelo, black walnut and yellow poplar. Softwoods that bond well include Douglas fir, ponderosa pine and sugar pine. Mahogany, an import, also bonds well.

The wood species that bond most easily include the following:

HARDWOODS: alder, aspen, basswood, cottonwood, magnolia, black willow.

SOFTWOODS: white and Pacific fir, eastern white and western white pine, western red cedar, redwood and Sitka spruce.

IMPORTED WOODS: balsa and purpleheart.

Contact Cement

Contact cement is used mainly for veneering and for permanently bonding plastic laminates (such as countertops). It bonds instantly on contact and is highly toxic. Because of the fumes, work in a well-ventilated area and wear respiration protection. It's best to apply contact cement with a brush or a roller to both of the surfaces to be bonded. Inexpensive, it bonds clear and is very moisture resistant.

DAP Weldwood Contact Cement is a brand of contact cement.

Glues shown above are, left to right: extended exterior wood glue; liquid hide glue; yellow exterior wood glue; white glue; yellow wood glue and brown wood glue.

Shown on the left above is a light-duty contact cement and on the right, a heavy-duty contact cement.

perature. White glues set quickly, but temperatures over 100°F can weaken a joint held together with white glue.

Known scientifically as aliphatic resin glue, yellow glues are the current favored choice with most woodworkers for most woodworking projects. Yellow glues, which come in liquid form, are easy to use and are great for a variety of applications, but as you may know from unfortunate past experiences, they don't work well for outdoor-furniture projects or for situations where a water-resistant bond is desired. Yellow glues dry translucent, are nontoxic, inexpensive and have a slightly heavier consistency than white glues. Not entirely waterproof, yellow glues are more moisture resistant than white glues and less affected by high temperatures.

Brands of white glues include Elmer's Glue-All. Brands of yellow glues include Titebond and Elmer's Carpenter's Glue.

> ADHESIVES CONTINUED

Plastic Resin Glue

Known also as urea-formaldehyde glue, plastic resin is good for cabinet repairs and for furniture that needs to be incredibly strong. A moisture-resistant adhesive, plastic resin is inexpensive and dries opaque. Plastic resin comes in a powder form that must be mixed with water and is toxic until fully cured. It also requires a lengthy clamping time.

Brands of plastic resin glues include DAP Weldwood Plastic Resin Glue.

Cyanoacrylate Glue

Cyanoacrylate is known generically as superglue and is used for quick, small repairs. Inexpensive, cyanoacrylate bonds to almost any material (plastics, metals, vinyl, rubber, ceramics and wood) and dries incredibly fast. It's fairly resistant to moisture and dries clear. This toxic glue comes in either a liquid or gel form; be very careful not to let it come in contact with your skin.

Brands of cyanoacrylate glues include Krazy Glue and Duro Quick Gel.

Resorcinol Glue

Incredibly waterproof, resorcinol is used not only for outdoor-furniture projects, but also boatbuilding and other marine uses. Expensive, resorcinol dries opaque and is toxic until it is fully cured. It comes in a powder form that must be mixed in a liquid resin and must be used within a few hours of being mixed. Although it's very strong and dependable, resorcinol does leave an obvious glue line.

Brands of resorcinol glues include DAP Weldwood Waterproof Resorcinol Glue.

Epoxy Glues

Epoxies are used to bond unlike materials, such as metals to wood or glass to particle-board. Expensive and toxic, epoxies are also waterproof and strong. Epoxies come in two parts, either liquid or putty, that must be mixed right before using and are toxic until fully cured.

Brands of epoxy glues include Devcon 2-Ton Epoxy.

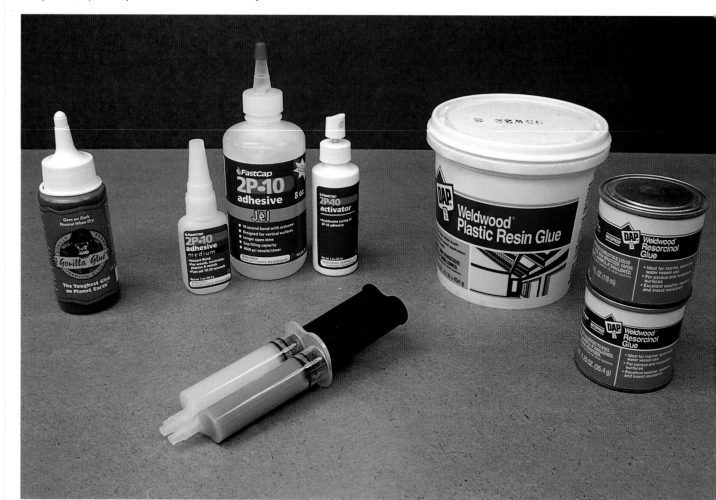

Shown above, left to right, are: polyurethane glue, cyanoacrylate and activator (speeds the curing time), two-part resorcinol and in front, two-part epoxy.

THE FORCES OF GLUE AND WOOD ATTRACTION

The American Society for Testing and Materials (ASTM) defines an adhesive as a substance capable of holding materials together by surface attachment. An adherend is a substrate held to another substrate by an adhesive.

Adhesion is the state in which two surfaces are held together by interfacial forces, which may be valence forces, interlocking action or both.

Valence forces are forces of attraction produced by the interactions of atoms, ions and molecules that exist within and at the surfaces of both adhesive and adherend.

Interlocking action, also called mechanical bonding, means surfaces are held together by an adhesive that has penetrated the porous surface while it is liquid, then anchored itself during solidification. The extent to which valence forces and interlocking action develop between adhesive polymers and wood adherends is uncertain, but both are generally acknowledged as essential for the most effective bonding.

Mechanical interlocking is probably the primary mechanism by which adhesives adhere to porous structures, such as wood. Effective mechanical interlocking takes place when adhesives penetrate beyond the surface debris and damaged fibers into sound wood two to six cells deep.

If an adhesive penetrates deeply enough into sound wood and becomes rigid enough upon curing, the strength of the bond can be expected to exceed the strength of the wood.

Wood surfaces may appear to be smooth and flat, but on microscopic examination, they become peaks, valleys and crevices, littered with loose fibers and other debris.

Such surface conditions cause gas pockets and blockages that prevent complete "wetting" by an adhesive and introduce stress concentrations when the adhesive has cured. Thus, the liquid adhesive must have high wettability, coupled with a viscosity that will produce good capillary flow to penetrate sound wood structure, while displacing and absorbing air, water and contaminants on the surface.

Pressure is normally used to enhance wetting by forcing liquid adhesive to flow over the surfaces, displace air blockages and penetrate to sound wood. This is where your clamps come in!

–extracted and revised from "Adhesive Bonding of Wood Materials" by Charles B. Vick, U.S. Forestry Department

Hot-Melt Glues

Hot-melt glues are used for quick repairs on leather or fabrics and are also good for making small repairs and filling joint gaps on furniture. Be careful when applying hot-melt glues, as the glue gun used to apply the glue can be very hot to the touch. Certain finishing compounds have been known to affect the strength of hot-melt glues.

Brands of hot-melt glues include Thermogrip Hot Melt.

Polyurethane Glue

Good for filling gaps and resistant to consistent presence of moisture, polyurethane glue is fairly new to the woodworking scene. In fact, it cures by being exposed to moisture: Polyurethane changes from a liquid into a foamlike substance when it is applied, expanding out of the joint. Its color varies from clear to brown, but it leaves a fairly colorless bond line.

One brand of polyurethane glue is Gorilla Glue.

Franklin International's HiPurformer glue is a hot-melt glue with polyurethane bonding strength and versatility with an initial set time of 30-75 seconds. Use it for a quick, clamp-free adhesion with epoxy-like holding power.

working with wood and glue

When you're mating joints using a glue or an adhesive, the first thing to do is make sure your wood surface is smooth, flat and free of any machine-caused roughness or chinks. Dirt or roughness in the wood will interfere with the ability of the glue to adhere to the surface. Be sure your wood is accepting of an adhesive and isn't too oily or dirty.

Your wood should also be dry, as water can dilute the power of the adhesive you're using.

Precision really is important when creating a glued joint. You can't rely totally on the power of the glue. For a successful edge joint, the surfaces that will be mated must match perfectly and tightly. This goes for mortise-and-tenon joints, too.

Be sure the glue is spread evenly on the pieces to be joined, but don't overdo it. Less can be more when you use adhesives to build your projects. The more squeeze-out you have, the more scraping and cleaning you'll have to do later.

Plan your glue-ups with an eye on the clock, and with some logic as to the order of the pieces you'll be gluing. Keep in mind that, depending on things like temperature and humidity, every type of glue has a fairly specific amount of time (1) it can be left open and exposed to air before you assemble your pieces and (2) it takes to set.

THE SIMPLE WATER TEST

To see if your wood is "accepting" of an adhesive and will bind well, drip a small droplet of water onto the surface of the wood in question. If the droplet remains beaded for more than 30 seconds, adhesion was not meant to be for this particular piece of wood. Inability to properly adhere is common with southern pine and Douglas fir lumber. The acidity of certain types of oak lumber and some Southeast Asian hardwoods also interferes with the ability of glues to join wood in a strong, stable manner.

If your shop is hot and dry, your glue will generally set more quickly. If your shop is too cold, the most common glues, such as yellow glues, often don't work well. Try to create an environment that is not too dry, not too moist and kept at a nice, midrange temperature, at least 55°F.

Clamps are an essential accessory to the glue-up process. Don't get too intense with your clamps and put them on too tight. Set them gently but firmly, and wait for the squeeze-out to appear. After it has set for about a half an hour, scrape off the dried squeeze-out. When using regular yellow wood glue, you'll probably want to leave your clamps on for at least an hour, then leave the glued pieces alone overnight for the glue to fully cure.

GLUE TYPES AND TIPS

When using polyvinyl acetate (white glue), spread the glue evenly and clamp the mating pieces together.

Aliphatic resin (yellow glue), the woodworker's glue of choice, should be spread on evenly and clamped. Because yellow glue has a thicker consistency than white glue, it won't drip and run out of the joint quite as much.

If you're using old-fashioned hide glue, be sure to apply it to both of the surfaces that will be mated and let both pieces sit before putting them together. The glue should be in a somewhat "tacky" state before you try to mate the pieces.

Be in a well-ventilated work area when using contact cement, as you'll experience strong fumes while you coat both surfaces to be mated. Let the contact cement dry before you mate the pieces to be joined. Contact cement bonds almost immediately.

Everyone knows that cyanoacrylate (superglue) dries in a matter of seconds. Apply it to both surfaces to be mated, press them together and voilà ! It'll stick. Just know that superglue, while it does bond a variety of materials together, isn't very strong or water resistant. If you're working with a porous wood, try the gel form of cyanoacrylate.

If you don't care about a strong, very visible glue line, and you're building something that absolutely must be waterproof, then resorcinol is a good choice. But it involves a little work. You'll have to mix the resorcinol powder in liquid resin and use it within a few hours. Once you've done that, coat and clamp as with other glues, but be careful, as resorcinol is toxic until it has fully cured.

If you're bonding unlike materials, such as metal to wood, epoxy works well, but does involve some mixing. A good gap-filler, epoxies have to be used within a few minutes of the mixing process.

COMMON ADHESIVES

ADHESIVE	ADVANTAGES	DISADVANTAGES	COMMON USES	WORKING TIME	CLAMPING TIME (at 70°F)	CURE TIME	SOLVENT
Yellow glue (aliphatic resin)	Easy to use; water resistant; leaves invisible glue lines; economical	Not waterproof (don't use on outdoor furniture)	All-purpose wood glue for interior use; stronger bond than white glue	5 to 7 minutes	1 to 2 hours	24 hours	Warm water
Contact cement	Bonds parts immediately	Can't readjust parts after contact; leaves unsightly glue lines	Bonding wood veneer or plastic laminate to substrate	Up to 1 hour	No clamps; parts bond on contact	None	Acetone
Superglue (cyanoacrylate)	Bonds parts quickly	Limited to small parts	Bonding small parts made from a variety of materials	30 seconds	10 to 60 seconds; clamps usually not required	30 minutes to several hours	Acetone
Epoxy glue	Good gap filler; waterproof; fast-setting formulas available; can be used to bond glass to metal or wood	Requires mixing; expensive; difficult to clean up; very toxic	Bonding small parts made from a variety of materials; bent laminations	5 to 60 minutes, depending on epoxy formula	5 minutes to several hours, depending on epoxy formula	3 hours and longer	Lacquer thinner
Animal glue, dry (hide glue)	Extended working time; water cleanup; economical	Must be mixed with water and heated; poor moisture resistance (don't use on outdoor furniture)	Time-consuming assembly work; stronger bond than liquid animal glue; interior use only	30 minutes	2 to 3 hours	24 hours	Warm water
Animal glue, liquid (hide glue)	Easy to use; extended working time; economical.	Poor moisture resistance (don't use on outdoor furniture)	Time-consuming assembly work; interior use only	5 minutes	2 hours	24 hours	Warm water
Polyurethane	Fully waterproof; gap-filling	Eye and skin irritant	Multipurpose, interior and exterior applications including wood to wood, ceramic, plastic, solid-surface material, stone, metal	30 minutes	1 to 2 hours	8 hours	Mineral spirits while wet; must abrade or scrape off when dry
White glue (polyvinyl acetate)	Easy to use; economical	Not waterproof (don't use on outdoor furniture)	All-purpose wood glue for interior use; yellow glue has stronger bond	3 to 5 minutes	45 minutes to 2 hours	24 to 48 hours	Warm water and soap
Waterproof glue (resorcinol)	Fully waterproof; extended working time	Requires mixing; dark color shows glue line on most woods; long clamping time	Outdoor furniture, marine applications	20 minutes	1 hour	12 hours	Cool water before hardening
Plastic resin (urea-formaldehyde)	Good water resistance; economical	Requires difficult mixing; long clamping time	Outdoor furniture, cutting boards; good for veneering	15 to 30 minutes	6 hours	24 hours	Warm water and soap before hardening

⊙ THE SIMPLE LIFE: SHAKER FURNISHINGS

The Shaker aesthetic has so intrigued modern Americans that the Renwick Gallery of the Smithsonian American Art Museum showcased their furnishings and lifestyles recently.

Shaker: Furnishings for the Simple Life was an exhibition featuring furniture and decorative arts from Mount Lebanon, the first and most prominent Shaker community. The exhibition is no longer on view, but the details of it profile the life the Shakers led.

This exhibition offered an opportunity to see objects created by Mount Lebanon residents for their own use and for sale "in the World," illustrating the principles of fine craftsmanship, order and simplicity embraced by the Shakers. Founded in New Lebanon, New York, in 1787, the settlement was the spiritual center of the sect, which, at its height in 1840, boasted 6,000 members living in 18 communities in the Northeast, Midwest, Kentucky and Florida.

VISITING THE SHAKERS

There are several Shaker museums in New England and the Midwest, in places ranging from New York to Kentucky. The Shaker Historical Museum in Shaker Heights, Ohio, is just one of many, but it's a great place to visit to absorb Shaker culture and history.

The museum is housed in a local mansion overlooking Upper Shaker Lake. It has a library and a museum shop, and features a collection of artifacts from the North Union Shaker colony.

For more information, visit www.ohiohistory.org/places/shaker.

Innovative and successful tradespeople, Shakers were celebrated for their functional, unadorned, and well-crafted furniture. They did not consider the products of their craftsmanship to be art but instead a palpable expression of their faith. In the words of one Shaker sister, "It was religion that produced the good tables and chairs."

In a communal settlement where time ordered all aspects of life, clocks were prominent features. The Renwick exhibit featured a tall clock from the Church family dwelling that dated from 1806 and was created by one of the first generations of Shaker craftsmen. While design influences from the outside world are evident, the tall case reveals the essence of the new Shaker aesthetic, where simplicity was key.

Of note to woodworkers, the Renwick show also featured a massive tool cupboard made around 1840, when Shaker design was at its purest and most abstract. This shallow cupboard carefully fit form to function. Designed to store woodworking tools, it is unusual for its size, asymmetrical layout, arrangement of doors and use of contrasting colored finishes.

Simplicity pervaded all Shaker products. Widely referred to as "Dorothy cloaks" after their originator, Sister Dorothy Durgin of Canterbury, New Hampshire, hooded garments were a specialty of Mount Lebanon seamstresses. Available in several colors, cloaks were standard dress for Shaker sisters, and fashionable with "nonbelievers" as well; Mrs. Grover Cleveland wore a gray Shaker cloak in 1893 to her husband's second presidential inaugural.

The Shaker movement began in England and moved to the United States in 1774. Led by Mother Ann Lee, the group members were called Shakers because of their early ecstatic worship practices, which included shaking, frenzied dancing, shouting and singing. Although they separated themselves from society, Shakers embraced the latest technology in their attempts to create, as they put it, "heaven on earth." Their communities are considered among the most progressive and successful of modern attempts at communal living. However, their numbers dwindled rapidly by the close of the 19th century, and only a handful of Shakers are living today.

The Shaker motto:

"Put your hands to work and your hearts to God."

⊘ THE FURNITURE SOCIETY

The Furniture Society is a tax-exempt, nonprofit organization founded in 1996. Its mission is to advance the art of furniture making by inspiring creativity, promoting excellence and fostering an understanding of furniture making and its place in society.

The society acts as a catalyst, bringing the field of studio furniture together. A quick visit to its Web site proves this out. You'll find links to news, conferences, collecting, a forum, society publications, exhibitions, a directory and a wealth of resources.

Known for its yearly conference, the Furniture Society offers a mixture of down-to-earth workshops on technique, heady discussions, invaluable tips and tricks, exhibitions, camaraderie, and, the group emphasizes, fun. These annual events are unparalleled as a way to network with others in the studio furniture field, whether you're a furniture maker, curator, collector, educator, writer, gallery director or professional, amateur or just plain enthusiast.

It's not necessary to be a furniture maker to be a member, either. As the society states on its Web site, "If your passion for furniture is something worth enjoying, whatever the aesthetic viewpoint, you deserve to be a member."

The society is currently comprised of

The Furniture Society logo

furniture designers and makers, educators, collectors, galleries, writers, international members, seniors, amateurs and students.

The online forum at www.furnituresociety.org is a great way to exchange information. The interactive forum exists to exchange ideas and information about furniture. You can join in the public area or, if you are a member of the Furniture Society, register for access to the special members area.

Members receive information about the society's publications and activities. You get the Furniture Society Resource Directory, which can be purchased separately for $10.00 plus shipping. Another book offered by the society includes over 300

THE FURNITURE SOCIETY

Box 18
Free Union, VA 22940
434-973-1488
www.furnituresociety.org
mail@furnituresociety.org

beautiful color images by different furniture makers; it's titled *Furniture Studio One: The Heart of the Functional Arts*.

Also now available through the society is *Furniture Studio Two*. Through beautiful photos and intelligent essays, *Tradition in Contemporary Furniture*, the second volume in the *Furniture Studio* series, explores the evolution of traditional furniture in contemporary work. Today's studio furniture artists seek to widen the vocabulary of furniture and expand its range of meanings. Yet even as they advance contemporary art movements, probe newly revealed functions, and incorporate such new materials as aluminum and acrylic, they remain within a still-unfolding tradition. In a variety of formats (scholarly studies, critical essays, profiles, reviews, design explorations) that see furniture from a variety of perspectives (personal, historical, aesthetic, social, economic, artistic, political), *Furniture Studio* has something for everyone.

The Furniture Society is a nonprofit that inspires creativity and promotes excellence in the field of furniture making.

CHAPTER **8**

> joints

when to use which and what they look like

The detailed part of furniture projects not often acknowledged or understood by the casual viewer, joinery is the stuff all furniture is made of.

Every woodworker has his or her own "comfort zone" and fallback joints they use time and again. But don't let joinery options intimidate you. Remember that each joint is simply comprised of cuts on wood, and if you're patient and willing to learn something new, you can utilize a variety of joint-making methods that can only improve and expand upon your woodworking repertoire.

Of course, there's no need to overcomplicate your projects. Use the best, but simplest, joint that is applicable to a certain project; don't make a super-fancy joint just to show off, unless, of course, you're going for a specific style, such as a mortise-and-tenon joint in an Arts & Crafts style piece of furniture.

form and function

When deciding which joint to use in a particular project, think about the aesthetics you desire from your furniture piece. What do you want it to look like? What kind of feel or style are you going for?

Sometimes the style of your planned piece will dictate the type of joint to be used, simply because a particular joint is indicated by a particular furniture style. Other times, that won't matter, and it will be up to the woodworker's own tastes.

Some woodworkers just plunge in with their biscuit joiner and make everything with biscuit joints, which are one type of

NO. O BISCUIT JOINT

entirely concealed joint constructions based on practicality and not prettiness. Other woodworkers like to implement more finesse and intricacy into their work by using exposed and aesthetically pleasing joints.

Often, though, you'll find yourself using a variety of joint types in a single woodworking project.

Most joints can be made with hand tools, if you consider yourself a craftsman and/or have a lot of patience and respect for the art of woodworking. Most joints, though, can be made with power tools, as well, which seems to be the modern method of choice.

Besides aesthetics, the strength you need from a joint is also necessary to consider.

Because wood is a living substance made of cells that absorb and release water, it moves, expanding and contracting due to moisture gain and loss. This simple fact is what makes joint construction a tricky operation, and is also the reason the simplest joints to create are sometimes the least strong.

Take the butt joint, for example. The butt joint has been around almost since woodworking began, and is the simplest method of joining two pieces of wood

BUTT EDGE JOINT

together. It's also the weakest, because it falls victim to wood movement and must therefore be nailed. Although better joints are in use, the butt joint remains popular because of its simplicity.

An evolution of the simple butt joint occurred with the invention of the mortise-and-tenon joint, which gives you a

very strong joint. If you leave the mortise slightly longer than the tenon, you give the wood in the tenon end room to expand and contract as it moves. Accord-

MORTISE-AND-TENON JOINT

ing to woodworking historian Gary Halstead, the mortise-and-tenon technique has been used on furniture pieces dating from the late 11th century.

Dovetail joints are useful when you need to join two pieces of wood that are

much larger and wider than the narrow wood pieces used for making mortise-and-tenon joints. Dovetails are made with 45°-angle cuts made on a series of fingers that

DOVETAIL JOINT

are interlocked for a strong joint. Advanced dovetail-makers are able to create concealed dovetail joints.

Bridle joints, considered a type of mortise and tenon, are visually pleasing and offer a large surface area that makes them easy to glue up. Two pieces of wood are interlocked

BRIDLE JOINT

in a T-shaped connection that is very strong.

Scarf joints, which depend on glue for their strength, basically are used to join boards end to end for length extension.

Illustrations of the variety of joints available to you are shown on the following pages. There are many lengthy books out there that show you how to make each and every joint. One good book is *The Complete Book of Wood Joinery* by R.J. DeCristoforo (Sterling Publishing Co., 1997).

WHAT THE JOINTS LOOK LIKE

NO. 20 BISCUIT JOINT

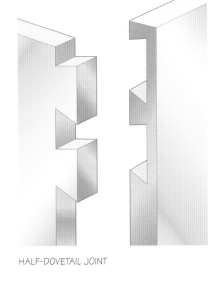

HALF-DOVETAIL JOINT

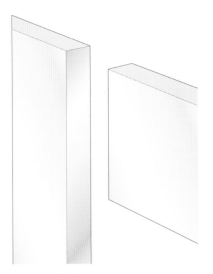

BUTT END JOINT

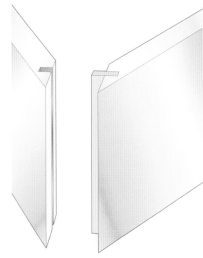

SPLINE MITER JOINT

STOP-DADO JOINT

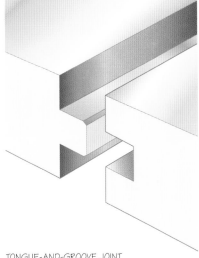

TONGUE-AND-GROOVE JOINT

DOWEL JOINT

END LAP JOINT

SPLINE END JOINT

END MITER JOINT

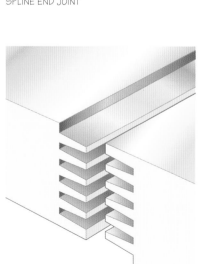

FINGER JOINT

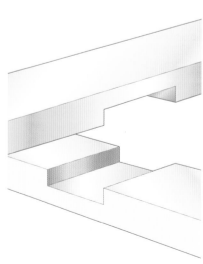

LAP JOINT

MORTISE-AND-TENON HAUNCHED JOINT

THROUGH-MORTISE-AND-TENON JOINT

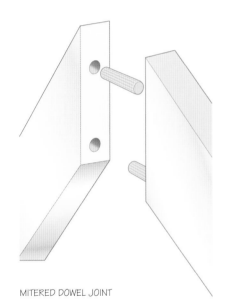

MITERED DOWEL JOINT

RABBET JOINT

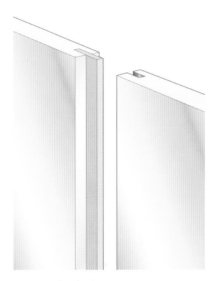

SPLINE EDGE JOINT

RABBET DADO JOINT

THROUGH-DADO JOINT

japanese joints

The art of joinery in Japan has been evolving for thousands of years. The techniques originally came from China. The joints shown here are just four out of hundreds that are used to build Japanese temples. These joints could be used as decorative joints to add a nice touch to a cabinet door frame or table leg joint.

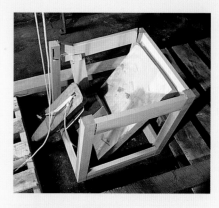

ANVIL'S AWAY!

In the August 2001 issue of *Popular Woodworking* magazine, the editors decided to perform a test to see which was stronger, a biscuit joint or a mortise-and-tenon joint. They rigged up a pulley to suspend a 100-pound anvil from the ceiling and dropped it on a small table made with mortise-and-tenon joints. The table cracked and caved a bit from the weight, but remained mostly intact and stable. They then suspended the anvil again, this time dropping it on an identical table, except for the fact that the joints were made with biscuits rather than with mortises and tenons. The table, much to the amusement of the editorial staff, basically exploded into many pieces. An admittedly unscientific test, the results nonetheless showed what many woodworkers have long believed: The mortise is stronger than the biscuit. But there are those who beg to differ from that belief. Some woodworkers swear by biscuit joints and claim that they are just as strong as they need to be, and that no one in their right mind would be dropping a 100-pound anvil on their side table, anyway, without expecting some major damage. For everyday furniture use, biscuits are likely just as good as another type of joint. One book attempts to prove this, and does so rather effectively, in the form of offering a variety of projects one would usually build with traditional joints and substituting biscuit joints: *The Biscuit Joiner Project Book* by Jim Stack (Popular Woodworking Books, 2002).

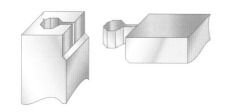

Otoshigama or half-blind dovetail mortise-and-tenon joint. Used in framework. The sheer strength of this joint is good, but it is a little weak at the neck of the dovetail.

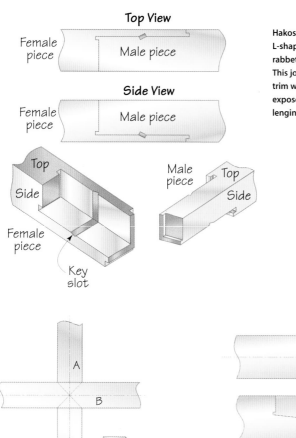

Top View

Female piece — Male piece

Side View

Female piece — Male piece

Top / Side / Female piece → Key slot

Male piece / Top / Side

Hakosen tsugi or L-shaped dadoed-and-rabbeted scarf lap joint. This joint is used on edge trim with its two surfaces exposed. A very challenging joint to make.

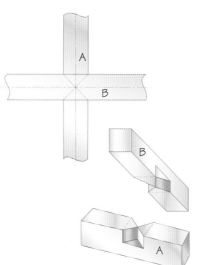

A
B
B
A

Tasuki kake watere ago or double-mitered cross-lap joint. Saw on the cross and chisel out the waste.

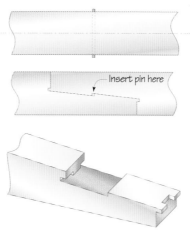

Insert pin here

Shiribasami tsugi, or blinded and stubbed dadoes and rabbeted scarf joint. This joint is used to join two beams. The joint keeps the beams from shifting side to side.

THE LINDBERGH LADDER LINK

Woodworking knowledge was the key to solving the "crime of the century"

If anyone ever tries to tell you that you're not using your time respectably or efficiently by working in your woodshop all day, and the furniture and other products of your endeavors aren't enough to convince them they're wrong, you can always pull this story out of your hat.

On March 2, 1932, shortly after Charles Lindbergh had become a national hero for being the first individual to fly solo across the Atlantic Ocean, his name was in the newspapers again, but this time the news was not triumphant. Lindbergh's 18-month-old son had been kidnapped from his second-story nursery window in New Jersey.

WANTED
INFORMATION AS TO THE WHEREABOUTS OF

CHAS. A. LINDBERGH, JR.
OF HOPEWELL, N. J.
SON OF COL. CHAS. A. LINDBERGH
World-Famous Aviator

This child was kidnaped from his home in Hopewell, N. J., between 8 and 10 p. m. on Tuesday, March 1, 1932.

DESCRIPTION:
Age, 20 months   Hair, blond, curly
Weight, 27 to 30 lbs. Eyes, dark blue
Height, 29 inches   Complexion, light
Deep dimple in center of chin
Dressed in one-piece coverall night suit

ADDRESS ALL COMMUNICATIONS TO
COL. H. N. SCHWARZKOPF, TRENTON, N. J., or
COL. CHAS. A. LINDBERGH, HOPEWELL, N. J.

ALL COMMUNICATIONS WILL BE TREATED IN CONFIDENCE

March 11, 1932
COL. H. NORMAN SCHWARZKOPF
Supt. New Jersey State Police, Trenton, N. J.

Known until the O.J. Simpson trial as the crime of the century, the incident received an incredible amount of media attention. It seemed that the police would not be able to solve the crime, until Arthur Koehler, a wood technologist at the United States Forest Service's Forest Products Laboratory in Madison, Wisconsin, began to investigate the wooden homemade ladder that had been used to gain access to the Lindbergh infant's bedroom window.

About 10 weeks after the kidnapping, Koehler was asked to look at some slivers of ladder wood that were taken from the scene of the crime. He was basically being asked to identify the types of wood used to build the ladder. After looking through his microscope, Koehler could immediately tell that it was a type of pine that grew in the North Carolina region.

He studied more slivers and narrowed down four types of wood used in the construction of the ladder: the North Carolina pine, Douglas fir, ponderosa pine and birch.

While Koehler began his research into the ladder, a ransom of $50,000 was paid to the kidnappers. Despite that, the body of the child was discovered a few miles from the Lindbergh home.

With no suspects in custody, the New Jersey state police went to Koehler again 10 months later to ask him to study the ladder itself. He studied marks left by the use of a handsaw, a hand plane, a chisel and a machine planer. He made calculations to determine saw kerf widths and sizes and shapes of the nails used.

Just as an example of the painstaking precision with which he pursued the matter, Koehler wrote to 1,600 lumber mills in the North Carolina pine region, providing them with relevant information to narrow down where the lumber could have come from. He knew that only planers having six knives in the side heads and eight in the top and bottom heads, spinning at about 3,300 rpm and feeding about 258 feet per minute could have dressed the board used in the construction of the ladder.

In the end, he testified in the case against Bruno Richard Hauptmann, proving such things as a relationship between the 16th rail of the ladder with a floor board from the defendant's attic. He proved this by showing that the rail was punctured by four square 8d cut nail holes that were not used to construct the ladder; these same nails fit the man's attic exactly, which Koehler said was a one-in-10-quadrillion chance of happening.

After a variety of other points proved, Hauptmann was found guilty, then executed on April 3, 1936.

A large part of the investigation required intimate knowledge of wood and woodworking, such as identification of species, distinguishing between artificial and natural features, and determining that pine rails came from young second-growth trees commercially cut in the Atlantic coast states, according to a Forest Products Laboratory report published in 1937.

Koehler said in an article afterward, "Just as a doctor who devotes himself to stomachs or tonsils or human vertebrae narrows down his interests to a sharp focus on the single field of his pet passion, so I, a forester, have done with wood."

CHAPTER **9**

> sharpening
angles and stones

Some view sharpening their tools as an unavoidable and necessary evil they'd rather not have to face. Others actually enjoy the meditative qualities of the repetitive task. Either way, tool sharpening is an intrinsic part of the woodworking process. It must be done if you want your tools not only to do their jobs, but do their jobs safely.

There's a much greater chance you'll cut yourself with a dull tool than a sharp tool. Not only do dull tools present a danger to your physical person, they present a serious danger to the quality of your work — instead of slicing cleanly through wood, dull tools will jerk and drag their way through the wood, leaving imprecise cuts and ragged surfaces in their wake. After you've grown accustomed to sharpening, you may even look forward to it. You'll find a parallel with another (often dreaded) woodworking task: finishing. Just like using sandpaper on wood, you will get best results by using progressively finer abrasives to sharpen your tool blades.

power grinding options

POWER GRINDING

Sharpening is a fairly precise science, involving proper angles and bevels. It can also be a lot of work, so it's not a surprise that the world of power tools has made its way into the sharpening arena.

Grinding wheels, also called grinders, are fun if you like to see sparks flying and fantasize that you're really a welder for a few minutes. They also can save you a lot of time and energy if you use them carefully.

Basically, you want to pay attention to grit and grain when buying a grinding wheel. Grinding wheels have thousands of little, abrasive grains distributed throughout the surface, which move against the tool to cut away metal. This is the sharpening process. Grinders are best for removing a lot of metal at once, when you get big nicks in your blades, for example. Of course, you'll still have to hone the blade after shaping the tool's edge on the grinder.

Dry grinding wheels are quite common in today's woodshop and are used for sharpening edge tools. Wheels on grinders are usually made of carborundum (silicon carbide) or aluminum oxide. In general, you'll find carborundum wheels on handheld grinders. Aluminum oxide wheels are used on benchtop grinders. Grinding wheels are available in a variety of shapes, sizes and grits.

Don't burn your tools! One thing you need to be careful of when using a grinding wheel is the tendency of a dry grinding wheel to overheat and burn the metal of your blade. Pouring water repeatedly on your tool to cool it down can damage it (by causing it to crack), so it's recommended that you place the hot edge on a piece of metal to cool slowly.

You can buy wet-wheel grinders, as well, which are slower and more expensive, but eradicate the worry of overheating your blades.

Some manufacturers recommend that you don't use dry grinding wheels to

sharpen your quality chisels or plane irons made of carbon steel. Wet wheels grind more slowly, but are kinder to your tools.

Woodworkers differ in their opinions about whether it's best to grind on a grinding wheel (known as grinding the bevel on a blade hollow) or to manually grind flat on a grindstone.

SHARPENING STONES

While grinding wheels are nice and will save you some labor and time, stones and files are also capable of sharpening your blade edges to incredible sharpness.

The options are almost infinite. Sharpening stones come in a wide variety of sizes, shapes and coarsenesses. First, there are waterstones and oilstones. Sharpening stone oil is a special mineral-based oil used to lubricate the sharpening stone and flush residue from its surface. This residue, which is comprised of a variety of materials, including the metal from the tools being sharpened, is called "swarf."

Woodworkers are best served by using waterstones, as oilstones are messy and more time-consuming. But be very careful to thoroughly dry your tools after using waterstones so they don't rust as a result of the moisture.

Waterstones are made of either aluminum oxide or silicon carbide and range in coarseness from 250 grit to 8,000 grit.

In your sharpening arsenal, you'll want to have a 600- to 800-grit waterstone, a 1,000- to 1,200-grit waterstone and a 6,000- to 8,000-grit waterstone in order to have a full complement of coarsenesses for different tools and sharpening tasks.

As the song goes, "Diamonds are a girl's best friend." Or rather, they're a woodworker's best friend. Although rather expensive, diamond stones (which have diamond dust embedded into the metal) last a long time and produce quality edges. They come in coarse, medium, fine and extra-fine coarsenesses. You can use fine-grit diamond stones for sharpening carbide-tipped tools.

Ceramic stones are another option. Less expensive than diamond stones, ceramic stones are made of aluminum oxide and are great for sharpening high-speed steel.

PROS AND CONS OF VARIOUS SHARPENING STONES

TYPE OF STONE	ADVANTAGES	DISADVANTAGES
Oilstones	Slurry not necessary Relatively inexpensive Available in a variety of sizes and shapes Easy to flatten Will not cause tools to rust Resist damage from tools (gouging) Uniform grit	Wear quickly Require flattening Finer grits are moderately expensive Messy / residual oil can stain wood Fragile Cannot sharpen carbide
Waterstones	Cut more quickly than oilstones Synthetic stones are inexpensive Available in wide grit range Larger sizes less expensive than diamond stones	Wear very quickly Water can cause tool rust Require a slurry in use Slurry can dub (round) edge slightly Must be kept wet in use Must be protected from freezing Relatively fragile Require flattening Susceptible to damage by tool edges Cannot sharpen carbide
Ceramic stones	Available in extremely fine grits Fairly long life Stay flatter longer than oil or waterstones	Expensive Will load quickly without lubricant Cut slowly Extremely fragile Limited grit range Require flattening Susceptible to chipping Cannot sharpen carbide
DMT® Diamond Whetstones	Cut extremely quickly Sharpen carbide Lubricant not essential, although helpful Water only, no oils Durable, long lasting Precision flat surface Stay flat in use Precisely controlled diamond crystal size Monocrystalline diamond only Highest value per dollar spent Double-sided 2-grit diamond stones available	Relatively expensive Require learning non-traditional sharpening method (light stroke only)

Data supplied by Stanley Watson, Technical Director for Diamond Machining Technology.

USES OF OILSTONES, WATERSTONES AND DIAMOND STONES

OILSTONES	BASIC FLATTENING, GRINDING OR EDGE SHAPING	INITIAL SHARPENING	MIDDLE LEVEL SHARPENING	FINAL SHARPENING	HONING OR POLISHING	STROPPING
Crystolon (oil-impregnated silicon carbide)						
100 Coarse	Yes	No	No	No	No	No
180 Medium	Yes	Yes	No	No	No	No
280 Fine	No	Yes	Yes	No	No	No
India (oil-impregnated aluminum oxide)						
100 Coarse	Yes	No	No	No	No	No
240 Medium	No	Yes	No	No	No	No
280-300 Fine	No	No	Yes	No	No	No
Soft Arkansas	No	Yes	Yes	No	No	No
Hard Arkansas	No	No	Yes	Yes	No	No
Hard Black Arkansas	No	No	No	Yes	Yes	No
WATERSTONES						
Japan # 800	No	Yes	Yes	No	No	No
Japan # 1000	No	No	Yes	No	No	No
Japan # 1200	No	No	Yes	Yes	No	No
Japan Finish	No	No	No	Yes	Yes	No
Japan Super	No	No	No	No	Yes	No
Strop Wheels	No	No	No	No	No	Yes
DMT® DIAMOND						
220 Mesh / 60m	Yes	No	No	No	No	No
325 Mesh / 45m	No	Yes	No	No	No	No
600 Mesh / 25m	No	No	Yes	No	No	No
1200 Mesh / 9m	No	No	No	Yes	No	No
6m Diamond Paste	No	No	No	No	Yes	Yes
3m Diamond Paste	No	No	No	No	Yes	Yes
1m Diamond Paste	No	No	No	No	Yes	Yes

BY CHRIS SCHWARZ, *POPULAR WOODWORKING* MAGAZINE

sharpening: plane irons and chisels

When I took my first class in woodworking some years ago, the first thing the instructor showed us was his shop-made waterstone pond.

With a reverence and care reserved for religious artifacts and small injured animals, the teacher brought the pond out from its special place in his cabinet. For more than an hour he talked with a furrowed brow about secondary bevels, wire edges and polishing the back of our edge tools.

All of us in the class did our best to stifle our yawns. I kept looking at the rows of chisels and backsaws and wondered when we were going to get to the important part.

Within a week we all realized that we should have paid more attention to the sharpening lecture. Soon there were only two sharp chisels in the shop for a class of 10 students, and we quarreled over them. Trimming tenons with the equivalent of a butter knife was no fun.

So I made it a point to learn to sharpen well. And I've been fortunate to be able to use a variety of methods, including: oilstones, diamond stones, waterstones, ceramic stones, sandpaper, electric grinders and the Tormek system, which has a wheel that dip in water as it turns.

Each system has its good and bad points. Some are simple, others don't make a mess, some are less expensive and most systems can put an astoundingly good edge on tool steel.

For me, the two most important qualities a sharpening system needs are that it must be fast and it must produce the keenest edge. I'll pay a little more and suffer a little mess to get a good edge in a hurry.

That's because I'm more interested in woodworking than I am in the act of sharpening. I have no desire to look at my edges under a microscope or fret about tiny imperfections in the metal. I'm not the kind of guy who wants to meditate on my power animal as I proceed up to 500,000 grit. I want to be done with it and get back to the good part.

FAMILIARITY BREEDS A KEEN EDGE

The steps I'm about to describe will work with every sharpening and honing system I know of on the market. That's because no matter what system you use, sharpening is about one thing: grinding and polishing the two intersecting planes of a cutting edge to as fine a point as possible.

The tools you use to get there are up to you. But here are a few words of advice: Pick a sharpening system and stick with it for a good long time before you consider giving it up. Many woodworkers that I've talked to jump around from system to system, trying to find the best thing (and spending a lot of money).

If you stick with one system, your edges will improve gradually as you get better and better at using your particular set of stones or sandpaper. Skipping around from one system to the next will only stunt your sharpening skills.

Second, please buy a honing guide. It's a big old lie that these things slow you down. In fact, these simple and inexpensive guides are quick to set up and ensure your edge will be perfect every time you sharpen.

However, don't buy a whole rolling army of honing guides. I use a $10 Eclipse-style guide (the gray-colored side-clamp contraption shown in most of the photos) for sharpening my chisels and most plane irons. I also own the Veritas honing guide. It excels at sharpening skew chisels and specialty plane irons that won't fit in the Eclipse guide, such as irons for shoulder planes.

Each honing guide holds the blade a little differently, and few of them are ever perfectly square. That's OK because what you're after with a honing guide is repeatability. Use the same guide over and over, and your edges will come out the same every time.

POLISH YOUR BACKSIDE

There are three sharpening operations that must be performed on all chisels and plane irons that are new to you. First you must polish the flat backside (sometimes called

If you don't polish the backside of your newly acquired chisels and plane irons, your cutting edges will always be jagged and easily dulled. You need to polish just the area up by the cutting edge. This is a process you'll only have to do once.

GRINDING THE EDGE

To begin grinding your edge, put the tool in your honing guide and adjust it until the cutting bevel is flat on your stone. Eyeball it at first. After a couple passes on the stone you'll know if you're off or not.

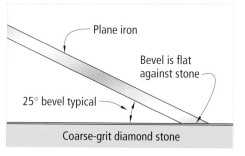

Flat-grinding your cutting bevel should not take long on a coarse diamond stone. If you're having trouble gauging your progress, color the cutting bevel with a permanent marker and you'll get a quick snapshot of where you stand.

When you're done grinding, this is what your edge should look like.

Plane iron

Bevel is flat against stone

25° bevel typical

Coarse-grit diamond stone

the "cutting face") of the tool. Next you grind the cutting bevel. Finally you hone and polish a small part of that cutting bevel, which most people call the "secondary bevel."

Keep in mind that these three steps are only for tools that you have newly acquired. Once you do these three things, maintaining an edge is much easier. You'll probably only have to polish the backside once. You'll have to regrind an edge mostly when you hit a nail or drop the tool. Most sharpening is just honing and polishing the

secondary bevel.

Begin with the backside of the tool. This is the side of the tool that doesn't have a bevel ground into it. It's one-half of your cutting edge so you need to get it right.

Start sharpening by rubbing the backside back and forth across a medium-grit sharpening stone or sandpaper. You don't need to polish the entire back, just the area up by the cutting edge. I begin this process with a 1,000-grit Norton waterstone, then do the same operation with

the 4,000-grit and then the 8,000-grit stone. The backside should look like a mirror when you're finished.

THE NOT-SO-DAILY GRIND

The next step is to grind the cutting bevel of the tool. You can do this on an electric grinder that has a tool rest, which will produce a slightly curved cutting bevel called a hollow-ground edge. Or you can do it on a coarse sharpening stone, which will produce a flat-ground edge.

Lots has been written about the advantages and disadvantages of each system. In comparing my hollow-ground edges vs. flat-ground edges I personally have found little difference between them in terms of edge durability.

I grind using a diamond stone for three reasons. First, it will never destroy a tool due to overheating (which can happen with electric grinders). Second, I use the diamond stone to flatten the waterstones. And third, the diamond stone is great for touching up my router bits.

I use DMT's extra-coarse stone for grinding my edges. Put the tool in your honing guide and set it so the cutting bevel is dead flat against the stone. Most tools come ground at a 25° bevel, which is good for most woodworking tasks. Mortising chisels should be set for 30°; tools designed for light paring only can be set for 20°.

Don't get too worked up about angles as you begin sharpening. Somewhere in the 25° neighborhood will be fine for most tools.

I use mineral spirits to lubricate my diamond stone. Most people use water, but a sharpening guru at DMT turned me on to mineral spirits. It evaporates slower than water and won't allow rust to build up easily on the stone.

Rub the cutting bevel against the diamond stone and check your progress. You want to grind the entire cutting bevel of the chisel or plane iron all the way across. If you set the tool properly in the jig, this should be about five to 10 minutes of work.

As you progress on this coarse stone, you should make a substantial burr on the backside of the tool. This is called a "wire edge," and you'll want to remove it by rubbing the backside on your finest-grit stone a couple times. Never rub the backside on your coarse stone. That just undoes all your polishing work there.

How you hold the jig is important, too. For plane irons and wide chisels, put a finger on each corner of the tool up near the cutting bevel and use your thumbs to push the jig. For narrower chisels, put one finger on the tool by the cutting bevel and push the jig from behind with one finger.

With the cutting bevel ground, it's time to refine the leading edge to a keen sharpness.

HONING: THE FUN PART

Honing is quick and painless if your stones are flat and you've done the first two steps correctly. The first thing to do is to reset the tool in your honing guide. Loosen the screw that clamps the tool and slide the tool backwards about ⅛". Retighten the screw.

This will set the tool so only a small part of the cutting bevel will get honed.

WHY I SWITCHED TO WATERSTONES

There are a lot of sharpening systems out there. And while I haven't tried every one of them, I've tried most. After much experimentation, I settled about five years ago on a system that used DMT diamond stones and oilstones. My system worked pretty well, but the oilstone part was slow, and my final cutting edge was always "almost" perfect.

Last summer I got my hands on a set of Norton's new American-made waterstones and it was like a door had been opened for me. These things cut wicked fast. And the edge they produce is darn-near perfect.

They feel different than many Japanese waterstones I've used. The best way to describe the difference is that the Norton stones give you different "feedback" as you sharpen. The 4,000-grit Norton actually feels like it is cutting (it is). The 4,000-grit Japanese stones I've used have a more rubbery feel to them, in my opinion. And they didn't seem to cut as fast at that level. The 8,000-grit Norton waterstone also provides great feedback to the user.

The downside to all waterstones is that they need to be flattened regularly. For this job, I use a DMT DuoSharp stone with the coarse grit on one side and the extra-coarse on the other. I also use this same diamond stone for grinding the cutting edge of all my chisels and plane irons.

The most economical way to get started with this system is to buy a Norton combination waterstone that has 1,000 grit on one side and 4,000 grit on the other. Then buy an 8,000-grit Norton waterstone for polishing. Norton also makes a 220-grit waterstone, but if you buy the DMT diamond stone you won't need it.

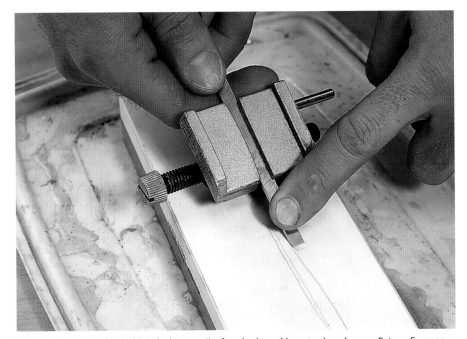

When honing narrow chisels, this is the best way I've found to keep things steady and square. Put one finger on the cutting edge; put the other behind the jig to move it.

Norton waterstones and the DMT DuoSharp stone are a great combination. The DMT handles the grinding jobs and flattens the Norton waterstones (800-446-1119 or nortonabrasives.com).

SHAPTON STONES: THE LATEST THING IN SHARPENING

If you think white-lab-coat wizardry is reserved for the manufacturers of power tools, think again. Some of the highest-tech science-fiction stuff happens in the knuckle-dragging hand tool industry: think unbreakable "nodular" cast iron, cryogenically treated tool steel and super-strong "rare earth" magnets that are incorporated into both tools and jigs.

And now the latest innovation is in sharpening. Shapton waterstones from Japan are all the rage among the sharpening gurus, who say the stones cut faster and wear longer than other stones. They also can be expensive. There are several grades of the Shapton stones, and a basic setup of three stones can cost you anywhere from $130 to $220 — plus you'll need some way to flatten them.

This speeds your sharpening greatly.

Start honing with a 1,000-grit waterstone, soft Arkansas oilstone or 320-grit sandpaper. I use the 1,000-grit Norton waterstone. Lubricate your stones as recommended by the manufacturer. Rub the tool back and forth on the stone. Turn it over and check your progress. You should see a secondary bevel appear up at the cutting edge. Rub your thumb along the backside; you should feel a small burr all the way across the cutting edge. If there's no burr, then you're not sharpening up at the edge; so continue honing until you feel that burr.

Once you have that burr, remove it by rubbing the backside across your 8,000-grit stone. Go back to your 1,000-grit stone and refine the secondary bevel some more until all the scratches on your secondary bevel look consistent. Use less and less pressure as you progress on this stone and remove the wire edge on the backside as you go.

Put the 1,000-grit stone away and get out a 4,000-grit waterstone, a hard black Arkansas oilstone or 600-grit sandpaper. Go through the same process you did with the 1,000-grit stone. Remove the wire edge on the backside with your 8,000-grit stone. At this stage, the bevel should look a bit polished in places.

Finally, you want to polish the second-

HONING THE EDGE

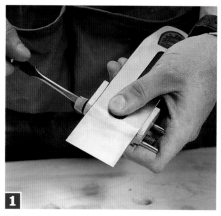

1 Before you begin honing the secondary bevel, loosen the clamp on your honing guide and nudge the blade backward in the guide about $^1/_8$".

2 Begin with a 1,000-grit stone and rub the tool back and forth across the work. Try to wear the stone evenly by moving the tool in a regular pattern.

3 After a dozen licks, turn the tool over and remove the burr from the backside by rubbing it a couple times over the 8,000-grit stone.

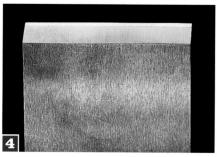

4 After honing the tool on the 1,000-grit stone, this is what the secondary bevel should look like.

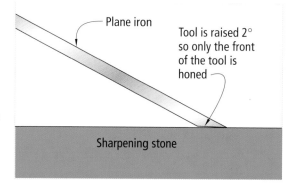

Plane iron

Tool is raised 2° so only the front of the tool is honed

Sharpening stone

ary bevel with your finest-grit stone or 1,500-grit sandpaper. I use an 8,000-grit Norton waterstone. There are Japanese waterstones at this grit level, too. However there are no comparable oilstones. A translucent oilstone is somewhat close.

Polishing is a little different. You're not going to feel a wire edge on the backside of the tool. Work both the secondary bevel and the backside of the tool on the 8,000-grit stone and watch the scratches disap-

pear. When they're gone, you're done.

Test the edge using your fingernail — see the photo for details. Some people finish up by stropping their edges at this point with a piece of hard leather that has been charged with honing compound. I don't find it necessary. In fact, if you're not careful, you will round over your cutting edge while stropping.

Remove the tool from your honing guide, wipe it down with a little oil to

MORE HONING AND POLISHING

5 Continue honing the edge by switching to a 4,000-grit stone. Remove the burr on the backside with the 8,000-grit stone.

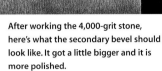

6 After working the 4,000-grit stone, here's what the secondary bevel should look like. It got a little bigger and it is more polished.

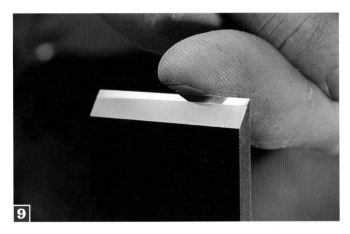

7 Repeat the same process on the 8,000-grit stone. You are almost finished. Tip: If your corners aren't getting polished, move the tool back $^1/_{32}$" in the jig.

8 Polish the secondary bevel on the 8,000-grit stone until it is a mirror.

Here's how to test your edge without flaying your finger open. Pull your thumbnail across the edge at about a 90° angle. If the edge catches and digs in immediately, you're sharp. If it skids across your thumbnail, you have more work to do.

9

prevent rusting and go to work on some end grain.

The tool should slice through the wood with little effort. And if that doesn't convince you of the value of sharpening, I don't know what will.

TWO JIGS FOR ALMOST EVERY JOB

There are a lot of honing guides on the market these days. After trying out most of them, I'm convinced these two will handle almost all your edge tools.

The gray side-clamp jig you see at every woodworking show and store is the workhorse in my sharpening kit.

None of these gray jigs I've inspected grind a perfectly square edge, but they're real close. Be sure to tighten the jig's clamp with a screwdriver when you fix the tool in the honing guide.

The Veritas guide (Lee Valley Tools) can handle many oddball tools. It easily clamps skew chisels, shoulder-plane blades, irons that are tapered in width and some not-so-stubby Japanese chisels. I don't use this jig as much for my run-of-the-mill plane blades and chisels with straight sides. It's much easier to clamp these in the gray side-clamp jig and go.

The Veritas jig will help you hone tools that would normally have to be sharpened freehand. It's a good investment.

SUPPLIES

- Items listed are from Woodcraft. Lie-Nielsen also sells the Norton stones.
- Side-clamp honing guide
  Item #03A21
- DuoSharp 8" coarse/extracoarse
  Item #140966
- Norton 1,000/4,000 waterstone
  Item #818263
- Norton 8,000 waterstone
  Item #822462
- Veritas honing jig
  Item #03B41

CHAPTER **10**

> finishing
sandpaper and finish types

Most woodworkers dread the final task: the finish. No scientific research has been done to answer why this is, but personal reasons abound: To some, finishing is just too frilly a process to sustain the hardened, weathered self-image of the stereotypical woodworker, and to others, finishing is just too time-consuming.

But if you can summon the patience and step into the finishing process with the knowledge that it's going to take some time, you can really make something special out of your project.

The finish you choose can either highlight the more attractive patterns in your project's wood grain or it can conceal its flaws. The finish also serves a more utilitarian purpose: It preserves your project for many years to come.

sandpaper

When you're finishing a woodworking project, you start and end with sandpaper. Although the serious sanding takes place before you apply your first coat of finish, you still need to use some elbow grease to buff and shine even after your final coat has been applied.

Sanding is done, generally, to prepare your wood surface for staining. When sanding, be sure to remove all wood fibers and open up the wood grain; this will ensure a penetrating, uniform finish.

Sandpaper made in the U.S. conforms to a system that grades the coarseness of the paper. You'll find sandpaper that ranges in grit from 12 (which is very coarse) to 1,500 (which is very fine). Woodworkers generally use 24- to 400-grit sandpaper. Use 40- to 50-grit sandpaper for smoothing rough wood surfaces, and 400-grit for the final sanding of your project's finish coat. Just remember, the smaller the number, the coarser the grit.

When moving through your grit sequence, try not to skip more than one grit. This will lengthen the life of your sandpaper and whatever implement you're using to engage it, and give you a higher quality finish.

Look on the back of a piece of sandpaper. There, you'll generally find the product number, lot number, abrasive type, grit size, open or closed coat and type of backing of the sandpaper. Sandpaper backing weight is rated by a letter designation. For example, J-weight cloth backing is lightweight; X is of a medium weight; and Y is heaviest.

TYPES OF SANDPAPER

Sandpaper comes in several types, which are manufactured for specific uses. These include the following:

ALUMINUM OXIDE: This manufactured sandpaper usually comes in an off-brown color and is incredibly abrasive. Woodworkers use it mostly for stripping old paint or varnish or for finishing hard-

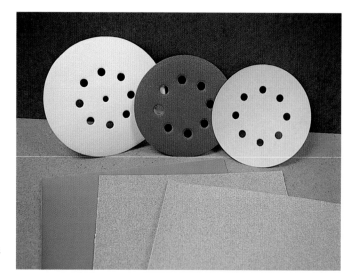

The back row shows a selection of sanding discs. In front, left to right, are: silicon carbide wet/dry sandpaper, garnet and aluminum oxide sandpapers. Thin, foam abrasive-coated hand-sanding pads are available for contour sanding and polishing.

The back row shows 3M Scotch Brite pads. These pads are also available for random-orbital sanders. In front, left to right, are standard #0000 steel wool and a steel wool-impregnated pad for a palm sander.

woods. It's also used for finishing some metals.

EMERY SANDPAPER: Emery is a natural abrasive, black in color and most often used for lightly polishing metals.

GARNET SANDPAPER: Garnet is a natural sandpaper, as well, and while it is not quite as abrasive as manufactured sandpapers, it's made a bit tougher from heat treating. Garnet is popular with woodworkers for finish-sanding fine hardwood furniture projects.

SILICON CARBIDE: This manufactured sandpaper is most often black in color and is the hardest of the commonly used abrasives. It's used for hand-sanding both softwood and hardwood projects.

ZIRCONIA ALUMINA: This manufactured sandpaper is most often used for heavy sanding, such as with a belt sander.

Always sand with the grain, not against it. If you sand against the grain, it will definitely show up when you put on the stain. And although sanding may seem like the

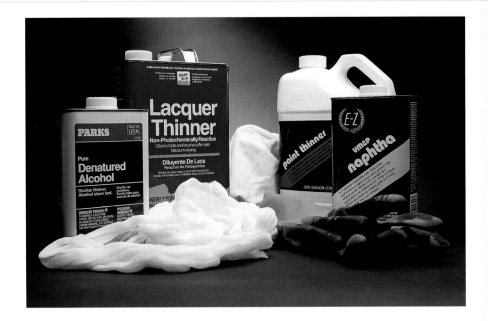

WOOD FINISHING TECHNOLOGY AND EDUCATION

The Wood Finishing Technology Program of Dakota County Technical College (DCTC) in Rosemount, Minnesota, is the only certified Wood Finishing Technology program in the United States.

The program has produced the country's best professional wood finishers, furniture restorers, spot repair artists and prefinishers since 1973. Mitch Kohanek, the instructor, has interned at the Smithsonian Conservation and Analytical Laboratory and is a member of the American Institute of Conservation. The program has been featured in magazines such as *Fine Woodworking*, *Better Homes and Gardens* and *Professional Refinishing*.

If you'd like to become one of the best furniture finishers in the country, you can find more information about attending DCTC on their Web site at www.woodfinishing.org or by writing to DCTC, 1300 East 145th Street, Rosemount, Minnesota 55068. Or call 800-548-5502.

most monotonous task in the world, it's incredibly important and not to be taken lightly. If you want a successful stain, you have to sand properly first.

Wood plus bare skin equals slivers. If you're sanding entirely by hand, invest in some gloves.

If you've joined the 21st century, not to mention the 20th, you can get yourself an electric sander, such as a finishing sander or a random-orbit sander.

HARDWOOD FINISHING BASICS

The first thing to do when you begin a finishing project is to prepare your wood properly. Of course, as mentioned, this begins with sanding. But this preparation process also includes removing any other serious defects you see, such as grease or indentations. If you don't have a smooth, clean surface to begin with, the stain and finish won't sink into the wood pores evenly.

The Hardwood Information Center (www.hardwoodinfo.com) explains that the cellular structure of a wood influences its appearance. Open-grained hardwoods (such as elm, oak and ash) are all ring-porous species. These ring-porous species have distinct figure and grain patterns. Close-grained hardwoods (such as cherry, maple, birch and yellow poplar) are known as diffuse-porous species. These species mostly have small, dense pores that result in less-distinct figure and grain patterns.

Note that some close-grained woods (such as cherry and maple) may have a ten-

dency to develop finishing blotches; don't wear yourself out trying to get these blotches out with heavy sanding. You can't get rid of them, no matter how much you sand.

When you get to the staining phase, the penetration of your chosen stain in a hardwood will ultimately depend on the final grit you used to sand the wood.

After your wood has been prepared by sanding and cleaning it, you might want to test your work. Before beginning the coloring process, sponge the surface of the wood with water, alcohol or any solvent to reveal any areas that might contain glue, marks or any uneven sanding.

For coloring, you'll find two main categories: dyes and pigmented stains.

DYES AND STAINS

Dyes are basically a mixture of colorants in mineral spirits, oil, alcohol or water. A dye will change the hue of your wood without concealing its figure. Dyes penetrate both

WHAT DISSOLVES AND THINS WHAT

SUBSTANCE	DISSOLVES	THINS
Mineral spirits (paint thinner) Naphtha Turpentine	Wax	Wax, oil, varnish, polyurethane
Toluol Xylene	Wax, water-based finish, white and yellow glue	Wax, oil, varnish, polyurethane, conversion varnish
Alcohol	Shellac	Shellac, lacquer
Lacquer thinner	Shellac, lacquer, water-based finish	Lacquer, shellac, catalyzed lacquer
Glycol ether	Shellac, lacquer, water-based finish	Lacquer, water-based finish
Water	—	water-based finish

> DYES AND STAINS CONTINUED

Did you know?

You can make your own wiping varnish by thinning any oil-based varnish or polyurethane enough so it is easy to wipe on the wood. This finish will build with each successive coat that is applied.

Shellac crystals are dissolved in alcohol.

soft and hard grains.

Dye particles have smaller molecular structures than the mineral particles found in stains. This is why dyes appear to be more transparent. Dyes also bind to wood naturally and therefore don't require an additional binder.

Stains are created from a variety of sources, ranging from synthetic materials to organic minerals. Stains consist of finely ground pigment particles that are suspended, or dispersed, in either a water-based or oil-based solvent. After the stain is applied, the solvent evaporates, leaving the color on the wood. Pigments are pretty easy to use and come in a wide variety of colors that can be added to other stains to increase color and/or density.

Stains can be applied in a variety of ways, such as spraying, brushing or wiping. You can manipulate the depth and final color by changing the length of time the stain is left on the wood's surface and how intensely it is wiped off.

Many woodworkers will color their wood project with a dye, then stain it, in order to avoid covering the grain of the wood with the saturation of a dark color. Dyes seem to stain the grain and the areas between the grain about the same color, whereas pigmented stains seem to fill the grain, leaving the wood surface with a little less color.

FILLERS, SEALERS AND GLAZES

In order to fill unsightly pores and smooth out the surface of your wood, you can use a wood filler. For example, oak and ash have large pores from their open-grained structure. In order to give those woods a smoother appearance, you can use an oil-based wood filler mixed with your oil-based stain to even out the wood's color and the wood's fill, all at once. Wood fillers can be heavily applied by spraying or brushing. Wipe off the excess with a rag or a scraper to make it flush with the top of the wood's surface.

You must seal the deal with a wood sealer. Some top-coat finishes are self-sealing, or you may need to apply the sealer separately. Often, vinyl sealers are used to lock in the color and protect the grain.

The top group is oil and varnish blend. They are easy to apply, but they cure soft. The thin coats don't provide much protection. The bottom group is wiping varnishes. They are thinned down varnishes, and are as easy to apply as the above oil and varnish blends. However, they offer more protection and can be built up thicker.

The sealer performs many functions: It locks in the color, seals the grain, begins the filling process and gives you a coating you can sand.

Glazes go on after the sealer. Glazes are basically transparent stains that are used to even out a light and dark area, as you see the true color of the wood only after the sealer has been sanded. Tinted applications of a sealer or top coat, called toners, can also be used to build up your project's color.

TOP COATS

Top coats come in many forms, from shellacs to polyurethanes. Each form has different preparation techniques and characteristics that you should keep in mind when making your choice.

Danish oil is easy to use but dries slowly. Amber in color, Danish oil dries to a satin finish and has low moisture resistance.

Lacquer dries quickly and is clear. It has a high gloss and is durable and resistant to moisture.

Polyurethane also dries slowly and comes in gloss, semigloss and satin. Colors range from clear to amber. Polyurethane is incredibly durable and moisture resistant.

Shellac is an economical, high-gloss and quick-drying option with color choices ranging from amber to clear. It comes in liquid form, as do all other top coats. It's affected by water, alcohol and heat, so is best for indoor projects. An even more economical option is shellac in flake form, as you can mix just what you need with alcohol and leave the rest on the shelf for future use.

Tung oil is easy to use as it requires no mixing and comes ready to use, although it does dry slowly. Satin in appearance, tung oil isn't very resistant to moisture.

Varnish takes much longer to dry than lacquer and comes in gloss, semigloss or satin. Amber in color, varnish is durable and resistant to moisture.

EXTERIOR FINISHES*

Failure of exterior finishes is usually the result of the wrong kind of finish being applied to the wood surface or of not following recommended application procedures.

Each wood product has unique characteristics that will affect the durability of any finish applied to it.

Dimensional change in lumber occurs as the wood gains or loses moisture. Wood in heated homes tends to dry and shrink in the winter and gain moisture and swell in the warm summer months.

Grain direction affects paint-holding characteristics and is determined at the time lumber is cut. Edge-grained bevel siding will hold paint well. Flat-grained lumber will not hold paint as well since it shrinks and swells more than edge-grained lumber and because wide, dark bands of

Polyurethane finish is one of the best for outdoor furniture, floors, tabletops and doors. If you want to make a wiping finish, thin polyurethane with mineral spirits until the finish is a watery consistency. This mixture is the same as paint thinner. Wipe on and wipe off, then sand between coats. Three coats will yield a highly durable finish that doesn't have a thick, built-up look.

summerwood are frequently present.

Paint will last longer on smooth, edge-grained surfaces. Penetrating stains or preservative treatments are preferred for rough-sawn lumber. These treatments often accentuate the natural or rustic look of rough-sawn lumber and allow the wood grain and surface texture to show through the finish.

Sanded and rough-sawn plywood will develop surface checks, especially when ex-

Shellac can be applied with a brush or sprayed. It dries very quickly, so multiple coats can be applied in a single day. When thinned, it makes a great polish for the interiors of cabinets because it will always have a slightly sweet smell when the cabinet is opened.

*COURTESY OF MICHIGAN STATE UNIVERSITY EXTENSION

CARE AND MAINTENANCE OF ANTIQUE FURNITURE

If you're the type of woodworker who doesn't conform to stereotype and actually enjoys the finishing process, you may find yourself collecting prebuilt antique furniture that needs care and refinishing. Here are some tips to keep in mind:

- Handle your furniture with care; don't drag around your antiques while wearing dangling bracelets or jewelry that could mar the surface.

- Even seemingly harmless light can affect the quality of your antique furniture. Some wood finishes, stains and paints are susceptible to fading or cracking if exposed to too much light. The heat from light can even soften a finish, thereby damaging it.

- Keep in mind that the original finish is part of the piece's value and charm. Don't just strip and completely refinish it without putting a little thought and research into what makes your antique special in the first place.

> EXTERIOR FINISHES CONTINUED

posed to moisture and sunlight. These surface checks can lead to early paint failure with oil or alkyd paint systems. Compared to rough-sawn or smooth plywood, medium-density overlay (MDO) holds paint well. MDO plywood is not always a stock item in many lumberyards, but it can usually be ordered.

MDO is a reconstituted wood product. Reconstituted wood products are those made by forming large sheets, usually 4' by 8', from small pieces of wood or pulp. Reconstituted wood products may be smooth or textured to look like standard lumber. Depending upon the basic wood component used in their manufacture, reconstituted wood products may be classified as fiberboard or particleboard.

Reconstituted wood products can be purchased unfinished, primed, with a top coat or stained. To paint hardboard and particleboard, follow good finishing practices as recommended for plywood.

PRESERVATIVES

Wood preservatives are not considered to be finishes. However, wood properly treated with a preservative can withstand years of exposure to severe decay and insect attack without being affected.

The common wood preservatives are creosote, pentachlorophenol in oil, and the newer waterborne salt treatments — all of which are restricted-use pesticides.

Creosote, and pentachlorophenol in oil, result in a dark and oily surface. Odor with creosote is a problem. Wood treated with creosote or pentachlorophenol in oil is not recommended for use around the home where people will come in contact with it.

However, wood treated with waterborne salts is suggested for use in patio decks, outside steps, privacy fences and other home uses. This material is generally light to bright green or brown in color. It can be used outdoors without finishing and will go practically unchanged or weather to a light gray.

WET SANDING AN OIL FINISH

Danish oil, which is an oil/varnish blend of finishes, can be wet sanded to create a satin to gloss finish. Here's how:

Apply the finish liberally with a brush, foam applicator or rag. Let it soak into the wood for 5 to 10 minutes. Add more oil in the areas where it soaks into the wood and gets dry. After 10 minutes, wipe off all unabsorbed finish. Let this cure overnight.

The next day, pour some oil finish on your project and start wet sanding using 600-grit wet/dry sandpaper and a flat sanding block. (On parts of your project that have curves or mouldings, you can simply hold the sandpaper in your hand.) Apply more oil as needed to keep the sandpaper lubricated.

You will begin to see a slurry form as you're sanding. This slurry will start filling the minute pores in the wood. Keep sanding until you see a satiny sheen begin to develop. Sand the entire project. Wipe off all excess slurry and oil, and let this cure overnight.

In the morning, you should see a very smooth and polished finish. If you desire a more glossy finish, repeat the above sanding procedure until the desired sheen is reached.

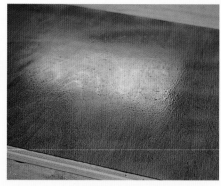

This photo shows what a wet coat looks like. It isn't pretty — yet. Let this sit for 10 to 15 minutes, then wipe off the excess oil. Let the finish dry overnight.

After the first coat of finish has dried, pour a generous amount of oil on the wood. Using 600-grit wet/dry sandpaper, sand the surface of the wood. The oil will act as a lubricant for the sandpaper. In this photo, only half of the wood is being sanded so you can see the difference between just applying several coats of oil and wet sanding each applied coat of oil.

The sample on the left was wet sanded twice and shows the built-up slurry created by the wet sanding. When dry, this finish is very smooth, as compared to the wipe-on-wipe-off finish on the right. It's important to remember that this type of finish isn't water resistant or hard. Although it does provide a finish that keeps the wood from drying out, particularly when used on solid wood.

COMMON STAINS AND TOP COATS

Stains

STAIN TYPE	FORM	PREPARATION	CHARACTERISTICS
Pigment Stains			
Oil-based	Liquid	Mix thoroughly.	Apply with rag, brush or spray; resists fading.
Water-based	Liquid	Mix thoroughly.	Apply with rag, brush or spray; resists fading; water cleanup.
Gel	Gel	Ready to use.	Apply with rag; won't raise grain; easy to use; no drips or runs.
Water-based gel	Gel	Ready to use.	Apply with rag; easy to use; no drips or runs.
Japan color	Concentrated liquid	Mix thoroughly.	Used for tinting stains, paints, varnish, lacquer.
Dye Stains			
Water-based	Powder	Mix with water.	Apply with rag, brush or spray; deep penetrating; best resistance of dye stains; good clarity; raises grain.
Oil-based	Powder	Mix with toluol, lacquer thinner, turpentine or naphtha.	Apply with rag, brush or spray; penetrating; does not raise grain; dries slowly.
Alcohol-based	Powder	Mix with alcohol.	Apply with rag, brush or spray; penetrating; does not raise grain; dries quickly; lap marks sometimes a problem.
NGR (non-grain-raising)	Liquid	Mix thoroughly.	Apply with rag, brush or spray (use retarder if wiping or brushing); good clarity; does not raise grain.

Top Coats

FINISH TYPE	FORM	PREPARATION	CHARACTERISTICS	DRY TIME
Shellac	Liquid	Mix thoroughly.	Dries quickly; economical; available either clear or amber-colored; high-gloss luster; affected by water, alcohol and heat.	2 hours
Shellac flakes	Dry flakes	Mix with alcohol.	Dries quickly; economical (mix only what is needed); color choices from amber to clear; high-gloss luster; affected by water, alcohol and heat.	2 hours
Lacquer	Liquid	Mix with thinner for spraying.	Dries quickly; clear (shaded lacquers available); high-gloss luster, but flattening agents available; durable; moisture resistant.	30 minutes
Varnish	Liquid	Mix thoroughly.	Dries slowly; amber color; gloss, semigloss and satin lusters; very good durability and moisture resistance; flexible.	3 to 6 hours
Polyurethane	Liquid	Mix thoroughly.	Dries slowly; clear to amber colors; gloss, semigloss and satin lusters; excellent durability and moisture resistance; flexible.	3 to 6 hours
Water-based polyurethane	Liquid	Mix thoroughly.	Dries quickly; clear; won't yellow; gloss and satin lusters; moisture and alcohol resistant; low odor.	2 hours
Tung oil	Liquid	Ready to use.	Dries slowly; amber color; satin luster; poor moisture resistance; easy to use.	20 to 24 hours
Danish oil	Liquid	Mix thoroughly.	Dries slowly; amber color; satin luster; poor moisture resistance; easy to use.	8 to 10 hours

NOTE: Dry times are based on a temperature of 70°F and 40-percent relative humidity. Lower temperature and/or higher relative humidity can increase drying time.

THE STICKLEY MUSEUM AT CRAFTSMAN FARMS

Historic landmark exemplifies Gustav Stickley's philosophy of building in harmony with the environment

Craftsman Farms, located in and owned by the Township of Parsippany-Troy Hills, New Jersey, is the former home of noted turn-of-the-century designer Gustav Stickley, a major proponent of the Arts & Crafts home-building and furnishing movement.

The log house, built in 1911, is one of the most significant landmarks of the American Arts & Crafts movement, and the site, which consists of 26 acres on the original 650-acre tract, has been designated a National Historic Landmark.

It is open to the public as a recreational site year-round, and the interior of the main house is open for tours from April to the middle of November. Craftsman Farms is also an official project of Save America's Treasures, a public-private partnership between the White House Millennium Council and the National Trust for Historic Preservation dedicated to the preservation of our nation's irreplaceable historic and cultural treasures for future generations.

Gustav Stickley, a well-known spokesman for the Arts & Crafts movement, combined the roles of furniture designer and manufacturer, architect, publisher, philosopher and social critic. A proponent of "a fine plainness" in art and the art of living, Stickley is best known today for his straightforward furniture, sometimes called Mission or Craftsman furniture.

Around 1905, Stickley moved his headquarters from Syracuse to New York City. In 1908, he began acquiring the property on what is now the western edge of Parsippany-Troy Hills, an area formerly part of Morris Plains, where he envisioned establishing a farm school for boys. The focal point of his "Garden of Eden" was a large log house constructed of round, hewn chestnut logs that were cut from the property's woods, and local stone, which was also found on the property.

Stickley originally designed the main house at Craftsman Farms as a "club house," a gathering place for workers, students and guests. In its huge kitchen, meals could be prepared for 100 people. The living and dining rooms, reaching 50 feet and warmed by copper-hooded fireplaces, made ideal meeting rooms. The porch opened to a vista of the farm and brought in light and air. The house is T-shaped, with a one-story kitchen attached to the rear. The large gabled roof has long shed dormers at the front and back, which allow for light and ventilation in the bedrooms.

A separate home for the Stickley family was originally planned to be built further up the hill. When Stickley decided that the school's opening would have to be delayed for several years, he modified the upstairs plans to accommodate his family (his wife, Eda, five daughters and a son).

Stickley designed Craftsman Farms to be self-sufficient, with gardens for vegetables and flowers, orchards, dairy cows and chickens. The produce grown on the farm was used in the restaurant operated by Stickley as part of his furniture showroom and department store in Manhattan. The property contains numerous support buildings including craft workshops, stables, a dairy barn, chicken coop, other farm buildings and three cottage dwellings.

Stickley and his family lived at Craftsman Farms until 1915, when he filed for bankruptcy after several years of financial difficulties. By then, the taste of the American people that 15 years earlier had embraced the clean, strong lines of Craftsman furniture changed once again and began to lean toward the revival of Early American and other styles.

Gustav Stickley made a lasting impression on American decorative arts. In a time when the crowded, highly embellished interiors of the Victorian Age were popular, his functional approach to design and his unornamented, clean-lined furniture introduced Americans to the modern decorative arts to come.

Craftsman Farms exemplifies Stickley's philosophy of building in harmony with the environment by using natural materials. To quote from Stickley's own magazine, *The Craftsman* (November 1911): "There are elements of intrinsic beauty in the simplification of a house built on the log cabin idea. . . . The quiet rhythmic monotone of the wall of logs fills one with the rustic peace of a secluded nook in the woods."

In 1917, Major George and Sylvia Wurlitzer Farny purchased the property in the bankruptcy sale, and their descendants lived on or owned the property until 1989. After Stickley left Craftsman Farms, the Farny family maintained the farm in Stickley's tradition, adapting certain interior features for modern family life.

When the property was threatened with a development for 52 town houses, the Township of Parsippany-Troy Hills, with the encouragement of community groups and others interested in the importance of the site, obtained the property through eminent domain. The Craftsman Farms Foundation is in the second phase of restoration of the main house to its 1910–1917 appearance.

The Stickley Museum at Craftsman Farms
2352 Rt. 10 West, No. 5
Morris Plains, NJ 07950
973-540-1165
CraftsmanFarms@att.net
www.parsippany.net/craftsmanfarms.html

PUT YOUR WOODWORKING SKILLS TO WORK ON A "HABITAT"

One of the world's most famous woodworkers isn't famous for his woodworking. Former President Jimmy Carter began his involvement with Habitat for Humanity in 1984 when he led a work group to New York City to help renovate a six-story building for 19 families in need of decent, affordable shelter.

That experience planted the seed, and the Jimmy Carter Work Project (JCWP) has been an internationally recognized event of Habitat for Humanity International ever since. Each year, Jimmy and Rosalyn Carter give one week of their time — along with their building skills — to build homes and raise awareness of the critical need for affordable housing.

The JCWP is held at a different location each year, and attracts volunteers from around the world. "We have become small players in an exciting global effort to alleviate the curse of homelessness," said Carter. "With our many new friends, we have worked to raise funds, to publicize the good work of Habitat, to recruit other volunteers, to visit overseas projects and even build a few houses."

Habitat is a nonprofit, ecumenical Christian organization dedicated to eliminating poverty housing. The organization has built more than 125,000 houses worldwide.

Volunteers, who come from a variety of backgrounds, from schoolteachers to woodworkers to building contractors, work with future homeowners to build or renovate houses, which are then sold to partner families at no profit, with no interest charged on the 15 to 20-year mortgage. The money from the sale of each house goes into a revolving Fund for Humanity to support future building projects.

Habitat invites people of all back-

grounds, races and religions to build houses together in partnership with families in need. It was founded in 1976 by Millard and Linda Fuller.

HOW DOES IT WORK?

Through volunteer labor and donations of money and materials, Habitat builds and rehabilitates simple, decent houses with the help of the homeowner (partner) families. Habitat houses are sold to partner families at no profit. Homeowners also invest hundreds of hours of their own labor into building their Habitat house and the houses of others.

Habitat for Humanity's work is accomplished at the community level by affiliates — independent, locally run, nonprofit organizations. Each affiliate coordinates all aspects of Habitat home building in its local area. Habitat's international head-

quarters, located in the United States in Americus, Georgia, provides information, training and a variety of other support services.

There are more than 1,900 active affiliates in 83 countries, including all 50 states of the United States, the District of Columbia, Guam and Puerto Rico. You can search for the local affiliate in your area by visiting www.habitat.org.

The Web site also gives other Habitat information, such as each country in which Habitat is at work, including progress reports, project descriptions and affordable housing needs.

▶ HENRY FORD MUSEUM & GREENFIELD VILLAGE OFFER A FURNITURE TREASURE TROVE

What could be more fun for the furniture aficionado than viewing artifacts such as George Washington's traveling camp bed or Edgar Allan Poe's writing desk?

You can do that and more at the Henry Ford Museum & Greenfield Village.

Located in Dearborn, Michigan, the museum and village make up the nation's largest indoor/outdoor history museum. They welcome over 1.6 million visitors annually. If you're ever in the vicinity, it's definitely worth a day, or several days', visit.

Touted as the finest documentation anywhere of the American experience, the Henry Ford Museum showcases the keys to the United States's growth and prosperity throughout its 200-year history, from hay-powered horses to "horse-powered" automobiles, from early steam engines to automated assembly lines, from a rough-hewn bench to the finest in upholstered furniture. Exhibits exploring all of these areas are found at the museum.

The museum's companion, Greenfield Village, occupies 88 acres and documents 300 years of America's past, where you can see, hear and be a part of history.

Early in the 20th century, Henry Ford began bringing together the original buildings from his family's homestead farm, then parts of his first workshops and auto factories. Eventually, these physical historical records were combined with other American structures that had propulgated such things as manned flight and electric light.

The actual homes, farm buildings, shops and businesses from America's history are on-site and open for exploration at Greenfield Village, often with real people interpreting roles of the original occupants.

The Stickley Furniture Company (1897–1986) is showcased at the Henry Ford Museum & Greenfield Village with records of the well-known furniture manufacturer, including income and expense records, patents, meeting minutes and design drawings that reveal how the company was organized and the evolution of

This maple and walnut highboy, belonging to Mary Ball Washington, the mother of George Washington, was once exhibited at the 1893 World's Fair.

PHOTO COURTESY OF HENRY FORD MUSEUM & GREENFIELD VILLAGE, DEARBORN, MICHIGAN

its furniture products.

"There are some amazing and interesting furniture pieces in the collection," said Henry Prebys, a furniture historian at the museum. "The collections (here) span the decades from almost the beginning of the English settlement in America up to the late 20th century. There is also a signifi-cant group of innovative mass-produced furniture. The 20th century includes a large group of home and office furnishings produced by Herman Miller, Inc. and developed by some of the most renowned designers of the period, for example, Charles and Ray Eames, Geroge Nelson and Isamu Noguchi."

Abraham Lincoln's rococo revival rock-ing chair, the actual one that he was sitting in the night John Wilkes Booth shot him, is also included in the Henry Ford Muse-um collection. The chair features its origi-nal bloodstained, faded red upholstery.

And, as mentioned, also at the museum is Edgar Allan Poe's rectangular, folding writing desk. Originally designed to be a portable desk, it has bail handles on the sides, with a top that swings down to form a flat, smooth writing surface.

George Washington's camp bed is also at the museum. While serving with the Continental Army, this was the traveling bed that Washington would sleep on dur-ing the American Revolutionary War.

The collection at the museum was begun by Henry Ford himself. He and his

wife, Clara Bryant Ford, had begun build-ing a collection of furniture for the muse-um and village by the 1920s.

According to the museum, agents, an-tique dealers and admirers urged Henry Ford to purchase beautiful, high-style pieces, resulting in a furniture collection that numbers in the several thousand pieces, and includes rare upholstered chairs from the 1600s, as well as modern Herman Miller furniture.

Other selections from the museum's furniture collection include examples of storage pieces designed to meet various needs, such as a high chest made in New England in the 1700s that found its way into the home of a Southern lady, who just happened to be the mother of the country's first president.

The highboy that once belonged to Mary Ball Washington has six trumpet-turned legs terminating in ball feet, and has both rectangular and square drawers.

Also in the museum's collection is a late-1700s cherry Hepplewhite sideboard with a mahogany top and maple inlay featuring eagles and shields. The introduc-tion of the sideboard signified a new trend in eating habits of the time. Until then, a family or person ate wherever they hap-pened to be, in the kitchen, on the porch or in the yard. But as dining rooms and a new entertaining style emerged that re-quired specific utensils, linen and other finery, furniture was created to store these items.

One cupboard at the museum tells a sad story. Hannah Barnard was born June 8, 1684. Her oak court cupboard on display at the museum was decorated for Hannah in Hadley, Massachusetts. It has her first name painted on the left door and her last name painted on the right door. The cen-ter panel between the two names is deco-rated with flowers, vines and leaves, all painted in black. The cupboard served as both storage and display with its wide, flat top available for expensive, imported vases,

This chair is from a parlor suite once owned by Abra-ham Lincoln's widow, Mary Todd Lincoln.

PHOTO COURTESY OF HENRY FORD MUSEUM & GREENFIELD VILLAGE, DEARBORN, MICHIGAN

pewter china and silver. The piece's design allowed Hannah not only to display her personal wealth, but send a message to let society know that she came to marriage with something that signified wealth and social standing. Married in 1715 to the widowed John Marsh, Hannah died 19 months later giving birth to a daughter, Abigail, who, in 1742, named her own daughter Hannah Barnard Hastings. The cupboard continued within the family until it found its current home at the Henry Ford Museum.

There are experts in the field of furni-ture currently on staff at the Henry Ford Museum & Greenfield Village, including curator Henry Prebys, an expert in Ameri-can furniture craftsmanship, style and design.

His fellow curator, Bill Pretzer, is an expert in the history of workers and their tools, inventions, industrial design and technical education.

For more information, and to find out how you can visit Henry Ford Museum & Greenfield Village, you can visit them on the Internet at www.hfmgv.org.

Edgar Allan Poe, noted author and frequent traveler, found this portable writing desk to be an ideal piece of equipment.

PHOTO COURTESY OF HENRY FORD MUSEUM & GREENFIELD VILLAGE, DEARBORN, MICHIGAN

CHAPTER **11**

safely setting up a shop

No one woodshop is the same as another, and no single set of layout plans will apply to every woodworker. The most you can do is plan ahead: Think about what you plan to use your shop for now and in the future.

You can save yourself a lot of time and headaches by arranging your shop the right way for *you* right from the beginning.

Not only do you need to think about safety in shop layout, you also need to think about arranging your floor tools and benchtop tools and smaller accoutrements, like hand planes and router bits, so they are all in easy reach based on the way you use those tools on a regular basis.

It doesn't make any sense to have your drill press buried deep in a corner that you have to dig it out of if you use that tool every day. A little advance planning can make all the difference.

think first

Setting up your shop in general and shop safety go hand in hand. If you set up your shop correctly, safety will naturally follow.

First, look around you. Where are you going to put your shop? In your basement? Your garage? A pole barn? A shed out back? Your living room?

Your available space and your building intentions will dictate, first, which tools you will choose to own and, second, how those tools will be arranged.

With forethought and planning, you can orchestrate an efficient, safe shop in the smallest of settings.

Of course, you can't be a kid in a candy store if space (as well as money) is an issue. Just because the guy down the road has an antique industrial-size lathe for sale for $20, doesn't mean you're the one who needs to buy it! Not unless you're going to use it as kitschy lawn décor.

Woodworkers with limited space won't be able to own big stationary tools. Hand tools and small power tools (maybe even a small table saw) will make up your woodworking arsenal.

Also think about the size of the pieces of wood you plan to work with. It's a good idea to set up your shop with outfeed tables, extra workbench space and other tables at the same height, so you can easily slide lumber from tool to tool.

The most basic safety elements you need are things like goggles (safety glasses), a push stick and push blocks, dust masks and hearing protectors. And, of course, use a little restraint and patience: Always read your power tool manuals before you start cranking up the decibels and stirring up dust.

SHOP LAYOUT CONSIDERATIONS

First, think about paint.

Most woodworkers don't stop to think about painting the interior of their shop, but it makes sense to address your walls before you start moving heavy equipment into the room. You don't want moisture in

your shop, and so it's smart to at least paint your walls with something that will seal up cracks and help the dust to glide off easier.

The point is, you don't have to paint pretty little flowers or powder-blue borders. Just think about the practicalities of a good paint job.

After you've addressed your walls, look down and think about the floor.

Make sure your workshop floor space is hard-wearing, void of things to trip and slip on, level, fireproof, easy to clean and dry. Most woodworkers have home shops with solid concrete slab flooring. If you want additional traction (like in front of a stationary tool), a cheap solution is to paint that area of floor with a rubber-type adhesive, sprinkle sand on it, and just sweep away the excess sand after it has dried. Instant traction!

Or, lay rubber mats in places for traction, or in places where you will stand often and for long periods.

And now onto the tools.

You'll probably have to make a few sketches before you figure out what will really work best for you and your available space. Draw the perimeter of the room in which you plan to work, make a list of all the major tools you plan to have and their sizes, and start rearranging the furniture on paper until you figure out how it all will fit together.

Machine placement is very important. Think about your projected work flow: Will you be planing lumber? Then running it through the sander? Or, if you're not a rough lumber person, will you be jointing edges and using a stationary table saw? Think about the process of your work, and which tools you use first and last in your building. Organize them in such a way that gives you smooth transition from one to the other.

Most woodworkers put their table saw in a central location in their shop, so they can walk right up to it and do their business, without having to navigate around benches

BOOKS ON SHOP SETUP

There are several books that focus just on setting up your shop. First there's Bill Stankus's thorough book, *How to Design and Build Your Ideal Woodshop, revised edition* (published by Popular Woodworking Books). There's the popular *Setting Up Shop* by Sandor Nagyszalanczy (published by Taunton), which goes into 220 pages of minute detail about such things as the advantages of a home woodshop, building a new shop, floor treatments, sound abatement, heating and ventilation issues, workbenches, storage solutions and safety.

Another book, *25 Essential Projects for Your Workshop* (published by Popular Woodworking Books), offers several tips to make your existing shop a more efficient and easier place to do your woodworking. It includes plans for such things as a router table, a table saw organizer, a lathe tool cabinet, a wall-mounted clamp rack, a sandpaper press, a tilting router stand and more.

Some nifty shop tips you'll find in *25 Essential Projects* include:

- Use five-gallon plastic buckets to organize your extension cords.

- Hand-dip your biscuits into glue before putting them in their slots if you're using a biscuit joiner to make joints.

The book also offers jigs and storage solutions.

and boxes and other tools. Think about 4×8 sheets of plywood, and other wood you'll be bringing in: Will you have room to move that around while you're working it?

You'll also need to keep in mind your lighting needs and your power outlets and what they can handle. Some specific tasks in the woodshop (and whether you're right-handed or left-handed) might require additional or adjustable lighting. You need to see what you're doing! You might want to think about installing lamps as side lights, or portable light stands that you can move around depending on the project you have going and its stage of production.

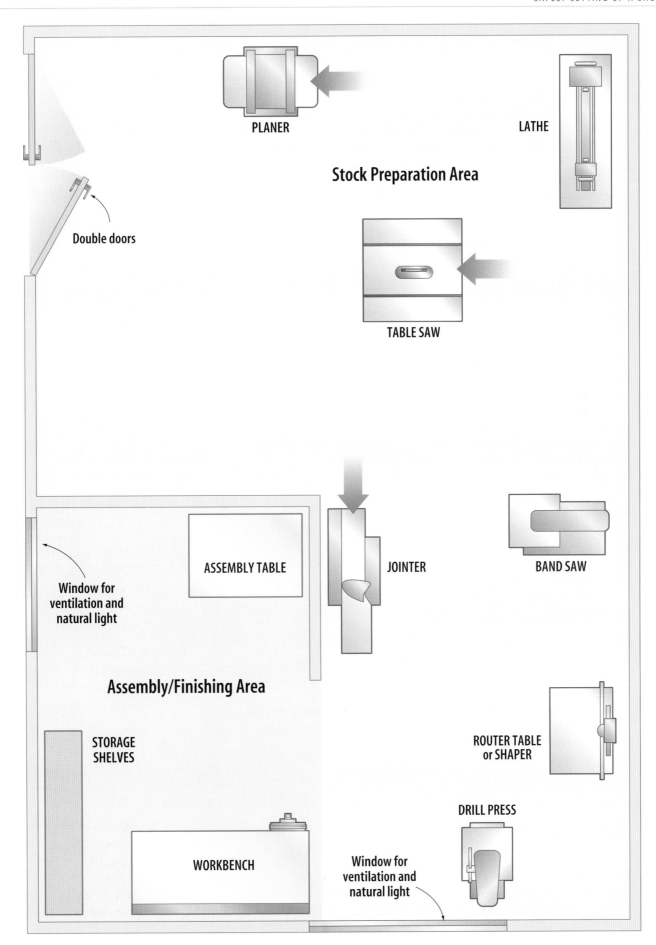

PLANER

LATHE

Stock Preparation Area

Double doors

TABLE SAW

ASSEMBLY TABLE

JOINTER

BAND SAW

Window for
ventilation and
natural light

Assembly/Finishing Area

STORAGE
SHELVES

ROUTER TABLE
or SHAPER

DRILL PRESS

WORKBENCH

Window for
ventilation and
natural light

safe and sound

ELECTRICITY AND FIRE CODES

Electricity and how it will be run through your shop can be a simpler problem to solve if you're just building a new shop. But if you're in the majority and already have a shop, as you add more and bigger tools that require power, you encounter new electrical difficulties. It's not something to take lightly, no pun intended.

You'll probably have to update your existing wiring if you're turning an existing building into a woodshop, or if you've recently added major, new tools to your collection.

Consult the *National Electrical Code* for specific guidelines, but be aware that many major cities will have their own specific codes set up. Refer to the codes implemented in your area for specific information and guidelines. The *National Electrical Code* is published by the National Fire Protection Association (NFPA).

Of course, where your major machine tools exist in your shop is where you need the most power. You're going to need 240-V circuits available for your major woodworking tools (such as stationary table saws and planers), as well as a good number of 120-V outlets for your smaller handheld power tools. And don't forget about your finishing equipment's power needs.

If you can, it's also smart to place your outlets high on the wall, at chest level or higher, rather than the usual low-to-the-ground placement. That way, you won't have to punish your back and your knees by stooping and bending all the time while you plug and unplug tools. Or, moving even higher, think about hanging outlets as a way to keep power cords off the floor, where you might trip over them.

Circuit breakers are installed in homes to turn off your electrical system if you're asking too much of it. If you keep tripping your circuit breakers while you're working in your shop, then you need to look at your wiring setup and your tool needs. Your tool manual will tell you the current

load capacity of a particular tool's motor. Then you can match your tool's needs with the *National Electrical Code*'s wire size recommendations for the expected current usage.

Electrical distribution equipment (which includes wiring, switches, outlets, cords, plugs, fuses, circuit-breaker boxes, lighting fixtures and lamps) were the third leading cause of home fires and the second leading cause of fire deaths in the United States between 1994 and 1998, according to the NFPA (www.nfpa.org).

More than 38,000 home electrical fires were reported in 1998. The main causes were ground faults, short circuits, fixed wiring, cords or plugs.

The NFPA recommends replacing or repairing loose or frayed cords on all of your electrical devices, including your woodshop power tools. Also, avoid running extension cords across doorways or under carpets; put plastic safety covers over plugs if they are within reach of children or animals; don't overload your outlets and always use light bulbs that match a particular lamp's recommended wattage.

Remember that all electrical connections in a woodshop for power tools should match the type of tool, as well as your shop's working conditions.

In order to protect the woodworker from shock and burns associated with power tools, all electric tools should have a three-wire cord with ground and be plugged into a grounded receptacle, be double-insulated or be powered by a low-voltage isolation transformer.

Three-wire cords contain two current-carrying conductors and a grounding conductor. Any time an adapter is used to accommodate a two-hole receptacle, the adapter wire must be attached to a known ground. Never remove the third prong from the plug.

Double-insulated tools are available that provide protection against electrical shock without third-wire grounding. Dou-

POWER TOOL AND ELECTRICAL SAFETY TIPS

To prevent hazards associated with the use of power tools, workers should observe the following general precautions:

- Never carry a tool by the cord or hose.

- Never yank the cord or the hose to disconnect it from the receptacle.

- Keep cords and hoses away from heat, oil and sharp edges.

- Disconnect tools when not using them, before servicing and cleaning them, and when changing accessories such as blades, bits and cutters.

- Keep all people not involved with the work at a safe distance from the work area.

- Secure the work with clamps or a vise, which will free both of your hands to operate the tool.

- Avoid accidental starting of a shop tool by keeping your fingers away from the switch button while you're carrying a plugged-in tool.

- Maintain your tools with care. Keep them sharp and clean so they perform the way they're supposed to.

- Follow the instructions in your user's manual that comes with each new tool for the lubricating requirements and for changing accessories properly and safely.

- Be sure to keep good footing and maintain good balance when operating power tools.

- Wear the proper clothing and apparel for working in the woodshop. Loose clothing, ties or jewelry can easily get caught in moving tool parts.

- Remove all of your damaged portable electrical tools from your shop.

–from the U.S. Department of Labor, OSHA

ble-insulated tools have an internal layer of insulation that completely isolates the tool's external housing.

If you need to use a temporary power source, such as during outdoor construction projects, always use a ground-fault circuit interrupter.

FIRE SAFETY

Every woodshop needs fire detection and prevention equipment. You should install smoke or fire detectors, and always keep at least one class ABC fire extinguisher in an easy-access location. And, of course, never, ever, ever throw water onto "live" machinery.

A portable fire extinguisher can put out a small fire, at least until the fire department can arrive. In the unfortunate occurrence of a fire in your woodshop, use your fire extinguisher if the fire is contained in a small area. Call the fire department and be sure everyone has exited the building.

The NFPA suggests you remember the acronym PASS when dealing with a fire:

Pull the pin. Hold the extinguisher with the nozzle pointing away from you, and release the locking mechanism.

Aim low. Point the extinguisher at the base of the fire.

Squeeze the lever slowly and evenly.

Sweep the nozzle from side to side.

Always be familiar with your fire extinguisher. Don't just buy it and hang it on the wall. You need to comfortably and completely know how it works in order for it to be effective in an emergency. Read the instructions carefully when you first buy it, and review them periodically.

Keep your fire extinguisher close to the exit. And don't forget to have a fire alarm installed in your woodshop, not just in your home.

UNGUARDED TABLE SAWS CAN MEAN SERIOUS INJURY

You can never be safe enough in your woodshop, and you can never have enough respect for what your tools can do.

One example of the seriousness of woodshop safety can be seen in a recent citation by the U.S. Labor Department. The Labor Department's Occupational Safety and Health Administration (OSHA) cited a manufacturer of wood products in Massachusetts for alleged serious violations of the Occupational Safety and Health Act following the death of a worker.

According to Brenda Gordon, OSHA area director for southeastern Massachusetts, the alleged violations were discovered during an inspection after an employee of the shop died. His chest was pierced by a small piece of wood that had kicked back from a table saw that was being operated by another employee.

"The inspection found that the table saw in question lacked the protective shielding necessary to prevent just this sort of accident," said Gordon. "The table saw should have been equipped with a spreader and antikickback fingers, attachments designed to prevent material from shooting back or out at operators or other workers during sawing operations, yet these safeguards were not installed on this machine."

According to OSHA, guarding deficiencies were found on two other machines, as well.

"A radial-arm saw had an exposed blade," said Gordon, "and was not installed so that its cutting head would return automatically to its starting position and was not equipped with an adjustable stop to prevent forward movement, while a jointer had a broken guard which exposed workers to its cutting heads during operation. These deficiencies exposed employees to possible amputation hazards."

The inspection also identified other hazards, including the use of frayed and damaged electrical power cords, lack of adequate training for a forklift operator and an inadequate respirator safety program.

Gordon noted that while the risk of amputation from unguarded blades and moving parts is often identified as a hazard associated with woodworking equipment, the possibility of employees being struck by kickbacks or ejected materials during woodworking operations is also a significant hazard.

"This accident exemplifies why machine guarding is a basic and necessary safeguard for saws and woodworking equipment and must be supplied whenever and wherever required," said Gordon. "Had this table saw been properly outfitted, this accident and its consequences could have been avoided."

If you work in a commercial woodshop and see violations, OSHA has a toll-free, nationwide hot line that may be used to report workplace accidents or situations posing imminent danger to workers: 800-321-OSHA.

And if you work only in your home shop, keep in mind how dangerous your tools can be if you don't respect them and use them in the safest possible manner.

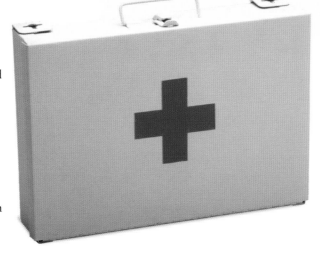

FIRST-AID KITS

Keeping a first-aid kit in your shop is a must. Whether you want to admit it to yourself or not, there's always going to be the occasional nick and cut in your finger, or maybe even just a really fat splinter. You need to have bandages and antibiotics in your shop to deal with those types of emergencies.

hand tool and power tool safety

Power tools can be dangerous things for a variety of reasons. This is a sometimes difficult concept for many woodworkers to really grasp, because the tools they work with every day become comfortable and such a common part of their lives that the woodworker can grow a little careless.

But you need to respect your tools and the power they have if you want to be a safe woodworker. Even hand tools can be dangerous.

Both hand and power tools can cause woodshop objects to fall to the ground or into containers full of chemicals, can cause objects to fly through the air, can create dust or fumes, or can simply throw wood chunks.

HAND TOOLS

The hand tools category includes any tool that is powered manually, rather than electrically or some other indirect way. Hand tools include such things as screwdrivers, wrenches, axes and hand planes.

Hand tools are most dangerous when they're not properly maintained or if they're not properly used by the operator.

The Occupational Safety and Health Administration mentions the following scenarios in which hand tools can cause injury or damage:

• If a chisel is used as a screwdriver (or vice versa), the tip of the chisel may break and fly off, hitting the user or others standing nearby.

• If a wooden handle on a tool, such as a hammer or an axe, is loose, splintered or cracked, the head of the tool may fly off and strike the user or others standing nearby.

• If the jaws of a wrench are sprung, the wrench might slip.

• If impact tools have mushroomed heads, such as on chisels, wedges or drift pins, the heads may shatter on impact, which could send sharp fragments flying toward the user or others.

Always direct your tools away from other people, such as visitors or family members, that might be in your shop while you're working.

Keep in mind that dull hand tools can be more dangerous than sharp hand tools. Keep your tools very sharp and in good condition, and you'll be a much safer woodworker.

And even though hand tools may look innocent enough placed next to flammable substances, they're not. When in use, iron or steel hand tools can produce sparks that most certainly could be a source of ignition around any flammable materials. If you'll be using hand tools around flammable material, be aware that there are spark-resistant tools available that

OPERATING CONTROLS AND SWITCHES ON HANDHELD POWER TOOLS

Certain power tools, according to the Occupational Safety and Health Administration, must be equipped with a constant-pressure switch or control, including the following: drills; fastener drivers; disc sanders with discs greater than 2"; belt sanders; reciprocating saws, saber saws, scroll saws; jigsaws with blade shanks greater than $^1/_4$" wide; and horizontal, vertical and angle grinders with wheels more than 2" in diameter.

Certain handheld power tools must also be equipped with either a positive on-off switch, a constant-pressure switch, or a lock-on control, including the following: disc sanders with discs 2" or less in diameter; grinders with wheels 2" or less in diameter; platen sanders; routers, planers, laminate trimmers, shears, scroll saws and jigsaws with blade shanks a nominal $^1/_4$" or less in diameter.

Other handheld power tools, such as circular saws having a blade diameter greater than 2", chain saws and percussion tools with no ways to hold accessories securely, must be equipped with a constant-pressure switch that will shut off the power when the pressure is released.

are made of nonferrous materials.

Even when using hand tools, wear goggles and gloves to protect yourself. And no matter what you're doing in your shop, keep your floors clean and dry to prevent slipping, an incident that can be doubly dangerous if you're holding a tool in your hand.

POWER TOOLS

There are a variety of ways power tools can be powered. Generically classified by power source, the main types of power tools are electric, pneumatic, liquid fuel and hydraulic. Most home woodworkers need to be concerned about the first two on this list.

Different dangers are associated with

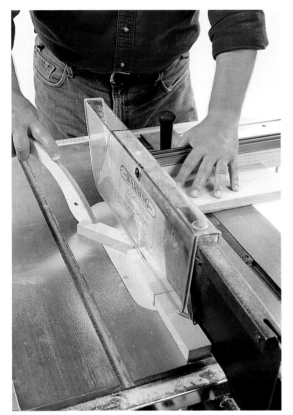

each type of power tool, but regardless of the power source, you should always use your tool guards, no matter what, and no matter how inconvenient they may seem to you. They're there for a reason.

Any exposed, moving parts of your tool need to be guarded. This includes belts,

WHEN CHILDREN AND OTHERS VISIT YOUR SHOP

Provide visitors, especially children, with safety goggles and make sure they're a safe distance away from machinery. Keep in mind that many machines (for example, portable planers) spit out waste at child's-eye level. If you have a workshop at home with children, educate them in the safe use of the machines. When not in the shop, remove start-up keys and lock the workshop. You may want to consider padlocking your machines.

gears, shafts, pulleys, sprockets, spindles, drums, flywheels, chains or any other moving parts.

And never remove your safety guards while the tool is in operation. Read the manuals that come with your tools.

Portable circular saws with greater than 2"-diameter blades should be equipped at all times with guards. An upper guard should cover the entire blade of the saw. A retractable lower guard should cover the teeth of the saw, except for the very location where the saw makes contact with whatever you're working on.

Electric tools can cause electrical burns and shocks, which can lead to serious surface injuries or even heart failure. To avoid this and other injuries, always operate your power tools wearing appropriate footwear; store your electric tools in a dry place when you're not using them; keep your work area well-lighted when working so you can see properly (this goes for when you're working with hand tools, as well); and be sure tool cords are out of walkways so you don't trip over them.

Pneumatic tools, such as drills, hammers and sanders, are powered by compressed air. Always wear eye, head and face protection when using pneumatic tools.

First check to be sure a pneumatic tool is securely fastened to the air hose so the two will not become disconnected. An added safeguard is a short wire or positive locking device that attaches the air hose to the tool.

Safety clips or retainers should be installed on pneumatic tools to prevent attachments from being ejected while the tool is in use.

TOOL SAFETY TIPS TO KEEP IN MIND

■ Read and fully comprehend all of the warnings and instructions that come packaged with your tools.

■ Keep your tools in good working condition with regular maintenance and attention. Don't use damaged tools.

■ Be sure your guards and antikickback devices are in good working order and in their correct positions. Before using a blade or a cutter, check to make sure it is sharp and clean.

■ Use the proper tool for the proper job.

■ Double-check your wood for loose knots, nails and other hazards. These can cause injury and damage your equipment if you aren't aware of their locations in the wood.

■ Always wear goggles, safety glasses or a face mask when using power or hand tools. When sanding, wear a dust mask, as well.

■ Never wear neckties, work gloves, bracelets or wristwatches or loose clothing. If you have long hair, wear a cap or tie it back.

■ Don't forget your ears. Wear hearing protection when using loud tools.

■ Be sure to have a push stick or push block within easy reach before starting any cut or machining operation. Don't put yourself in awkward positions in which a sudden slip could make your hand hit the blade or cutter.

Pneumatic tools that shoot nails, rivets, staples or other fasteners, and operate at a pressure of more than 100 pounds per square inch, have to be equipped with a special device that keeps the fasteners from being ejected unless the muzzle is being pressed against the work surface.

Of course, just like with real guns, never point a compressed air gun at anyone.

And as you probably know, pneumatic tools are often very noisy. Remember always to wear hearing protection.

dust collection and ventilation

Since wood dust is a natural substance, people are often surprised to learn that wood dust is an incredibly dangerous, not to mention irritating, substance.

It can make you cough, make your eyes tear up, even make you feel a little nauseous, if you breathe in too much or the wrong type. These minor things mostly cause the woodworker short-term irritation, but wood dust can also be a serious health concern. It's possible that it can cause respiratory problems and even cancer. And aside from the dust that can accumulate in your body, wood dust can also be the cause of fire and explosions.

So take your dust-collection accessories very seriously. They're not frivolous or extraneous additions to your shop; good dust collection is a necessity.

Wood dust is produced pretty much any time you're doing anything with wood in your shop: It's produced from chipping, sawing, turning, drilling, sanding, planing and jointing. Sanding is the worst perpetrator because the particles produced are so small that masks often don't filter everything, allowing tiny dust particles to enter the woodworker's unsuspecting nasal cavities, sinuses and lungs.

And although hardwoods such as beech, oak and mahogany have been documented to be more dangerous (they produce very fine particles of dust and have links to certain nasal cancers), one of the most hazardous woods is the softwood known as western red cedar. Other softwoods, such as pine, pose less of a risk. Medium-density fiberboard (MDF) is unhealthy for humans because of the bonding agent used, and should be regarded in terms of dust danger the same as a hardwood.

A variety of factors are thought to contribute to the reasons wood dust is unhealthy for humans, including the amount of tannin in the wood, but new studies in this field are being conducted all of the time, and much is still to be discovered.

The best defense against wood dust in your body is a properly designed and maintained exhaust system to collect the dust that is produced in your shop. And you should use dust respirators, especially if, for some reason, you do not have a good exhaust system installed.

According to the Health and Safety Executive (HSE) of England, too much dust of any kind can adversely affect health in a variety of ways: skin disorders, nose obstructions, asthma and a rare type of nasal cancer. The HSE goes on to say that concentrations of small dust particles in the air can form a mixture that will explode if ignited, and wood dust burns readily if ignited. Fires can start because of a variety of reasons, such as badly maintained heating units, overheated electric motors, electric sparks flying or cigarettes. Just one more reason to stop smoking, especially when you're working wood.

Slightly less dramatic, but just as serious, is the possibility of slipping or tripping from an accumulation of wood dust on the floor. So keep your floors clear.

Always have on hand personal protective equipment, such as goggles or other eyewear, overalls and gloves. Although laundry isn't a woodworker's favorite task, you need to wash your woodworking clothing regularly to prevent heavy dust accumulation.

To control your exposure to airborne dust in your woodshop, do the following: Try to use a process that reduces the generation of dust in the first place; have local exhaust ventilation attached to all woodworking machines to prevent dust from entering your shop altogether; and, of course, be sure the equipment you have is in proper working order and always maintained.

When you go shopping for your dust-collection units, know that you'll be looking at five different categories: shop vacuums and single-stage, two-stage and cyclone dust collectors, as well as air cleaners that are installed near the ceiling to filter and trap dust particles.

A great reference for comparing and contrasting the different types of dust collectors available is *The Insider's Guide to Buying Tools*, published by Popular Woodworking Books. It describes the features, prices and uses of many different types of dust collectors.

WOODTURNING: ONE OF AMERICA'S MOST POPULAR CRAFTS

The Renwick Gallery of the Smithsonian American Art Museum celebrated the variety and beauty of woodturning, one of the most popular craft art techniques today, in *Wood Turning Since 1930*, an exhibition that traces the evolution of the craft from a functional hobby in the 1930s through the experimentation of the craft revival during World War II to the sophisticated art form of today.

"Woodturning is a fascinating movement because it is rich with a long history and great variety," said Kenneth Trapp, curator-in-charge of the Renwick Gallery. "The 130 objects in this exhibition demonstrated how this simple hobby has grown to encompass both the functional and the unconventional, including expressive qualities such as color and sculptural forms."

The exhibition, *Compote* (about 1940s) by Carl Huskey, represented the earliest trend in woodturning, one that was practiced in high school shop classes, factories and by hobbyists. Constructed of three separately turned parts, the simple and sleek conventional form is indicative of the early tradition.

Studio turning began in the late 1930s with James Prestini and Bob Stocksdale who began creating more stylistic pieces. Turned objects such as Prestini's *Salad Set* (1939) encouraged later woodturners to abandon the traditional form in favor of experimentation. Prestini's functional tableware is designed to appear as sculpture with seven small, identical bowls that fit perfectly alongside one another. He continues to employ a simple shape, but uses a new scraping technique and lacquer for a thinner and smoother surface.

Rude Osolnik takes Prestini's experimentation a step further. In his own *Salad Set* (about 1950) Osolnik deviates from Prestini's precise approach, instead turning his set of rosewood bowls to have asymmetrical, individualistic shapes.

Since the 1950s, woodturners have continued to deviate from conventional wood-

Pictured above is James Prestini's "Salad Set" from 1939. Studio turning began in the late 1930s with Prestini and Bob Stockdale. Turned objects such as the set above encouraged later woodturners to transition from traditional forms in favor of experimentation. Famed turner Rude Osolnik took Prestini's method a bit further. In his own "Salad Set" (about 1950), Osolnik deviates from Prestini's precise approach — turning his set of rosewood bowls to have asymmetrical, individualistic shapes.

working. Giles Gilson does so by incorporating color in *Sunset* (1987), applying bright orange and yellow enamel paint to represent a southwestern sunset. The striped pattern on the surface suggests southwestern pottery or striping on cars.

Michael Hosaluk is one of the first woodturners to incorporate paint, mixed media and found objects into his work. In *Tribal Gathering* (1991) he creates a free-standing sculptural form created from linen thread, paint and beads that makes reference to aboriginal ritual objects.

Craig Nutt's *Radish Salad Bowl* (1998) is a playful, witty sculpture that at the same time acts as functional serving ware. It is a salad bowl on a stand with oversize yellow peppers as legs, bright red radishes as salad bowls and radish leaves as tossers. In this work, Nutt creates rough shapes with the lathe and later shapes his forms by hand.

The exhibition was organized by the Wood Turning Center, Philadelphia, and the Yale University Art Gallery, New Haven, Connecticut.

WHICH TYPE ARE YOU?

There are two types of woodturners out there: those who grudgingly turn to the lathe (no pun intended) when they're forced to make a chair spindle, and those who never leave the lathe and turn out (again, no pun intended) artistically crafted bowls, pens and vases.

If you're in the latter group, contact the American Association of Woodturners (AAW).

If you become a member of AAW, you'll be joining 8,700 other enthusiasts from around the world.

When you go to the AAW Web site (www.woodturner.org), you can view a gallery of members' turned art, see a calendar of upcoming events, learn about AAW's annual symposium, and much more.

⊙ sources AND supplies

The following Internet addresses were accurate when these pages were written, but Web sites change frequently. If you can't find a site listed, try a search engine such as www.google.com to find the correct address. Also, although most Web addresses are not case sensitive, a few are; thus, any uppercase letters that appear in the addresses listed are necessary.

If you do not have Internet access at home, try your local public library.

BOOKS AND MAGAZINES

AMATEUR WOODWORKER
www.am-wood.com

AMERICAN WOODWORKER MAGAZINE
www.americanwoodworker.com

FINE WOODWORKING
www.taunton.com

HANDY MAGAZINE
visitors.handymanclub.com

POPULAR WOODWORKING MAGAZINE
www.popwood.com

SHOPNOTES MAGAZINE
www.shopnotes.com

WOOD MAGAZINE
www.woodmagazine.com

WOODSHOP NEWS
www.woodshopnews.com

WOODSMITH MAGAZINE
www.woodsmith.com

WOODWORKER'S JOURNAL
www.woodworkersjournal.com

WORKBENCH MAGAZINE
www.workbenchmagazine.com

SHOPPING

3M CORPORATION
www.3m.com

84 LUMBER
www.84lumber.com

ACE HARDWARE
www.acehardware.com

ADAMS & KENNEDY – THE WOODSOURCE
www.wood-source.com

ADJUSTABLE CLAMP COMPANY
www.adjustableclamp.com

AIR HANDLING SYSTEMS
www.airhand.com

BALL AND BALL ANTIQUE HARDWARE REPRODUCTIONS
www.ballandball-us.com

BELSAW COMPANY
www.belsaw.com

BIESEMEYER WOODWORKING TOOLS
www.biesemeyer.com

BLACK & DECKER, INC.
www.blackanddecker.com

BOSCH
www.boschtools.com

CAMPELL HAUSFELD
www.chpower.com

CARBA-TEC
www.carbatec.com.au

CMT USA, INC.
www.cmtusa.com

COLEMAN POWERMATE
www.powermate.com/coleman

COOPER TOOLS
www.coopertools.com

CONSTANTINES WOOD CENTER
www.constantines.com

C.P. MACHINE TOOLS, INC.
www.cptools.com

CRAFTSMAN TOOLS — SEARS
www.sears.com/craftsman

DELTA MACHINERY
www.deltawoodworking.com

DEVILBISS AIR POWER COMPANY
www.devap.com

DEWALT
www.dewalt.com

DIAMOND MACHINING TECHNOLOGY, INC (DMT)
www.dmtsharp.com

DOUG MOCKETT & COMPANY, INC.
www.mockett.com

DREMEL
www.dremel.com

DUO-FAST
www.duo-fast.com

DYNABRADE INDUSTRIAL POWER TOOLS
www.dynabrade.com

ECOGATE, INC.
www.ecogate.com

EMGLO AIR COMPRESSORS
www.emglo.com

> SOURCES AND SUPPLIES CONTINUED

EXAKTOR PRECISION WOODWORKING TOOLS, INC.
www.excal-tools.com

EXCALIBUR TOOLS
www.excalibur-tools.com

FEIN POWER TOOLS
www.fein.com

FESTOOL
www.festool.com

FORREST MANUFACTURING COMPANY, INC.
forrest.woodmall.com

FREUD, INC.
www.freudtools.com

FROG TOOL
www.greatamericantool.com

GARRETT WADE CO., INC.
www.garrettwade.com

GENERAL INTERNATIONAL MFG. CO. LTD.
www.general.ca

GORILLA GLUE
www.gorillaglue.com

GREAT AMERICAN TOOL COMPANY, INC.
www.greatamericantool.com

GRIZZLY INDUSTRIAL, INC.
www.grizzlyindustrial.com

HARDWARE HUT
www.thehardwarehut.com

HARTVILLE TOOL
www.hartvilletool.com

HEGNER — ADVANCED MACHINERY
www.advmachinery.com

HITACHI POWER TOOLS
www.hitachi.com

HORTON BRASSES, INC.
www.horton-brasses.com

THE HOME DEPOT
www.homedepot.com

INGERSOLL-RAND
www.ingersoll-rand.com

JAPAN WOODWORKER CATALOG
www.japanwoodworker.com

JESSEM TOOL COMPANY
www.jessem.com

JET
www.jettools.com

KLINGSPOR'S WOODWORKING SHOP
www.woodworkingshop.com

LAGUNA TOOLS
www.lagunatools.com

LAMELLO — COLONIAL SAW, INC.
www.csaw.com

LEE VALLEY TOOLS, LTD.
www.leevalley.com

LENEAVE MACHINERY & SUPPLY COMPANY
800-442-2302

LIE-NIELSEN TOOLWORKS, INC.
www.lie-nielsen.com

LOBO MACHINERY CORPORATION
www.lobomachine.com

LOWE'S HOME IMPROVEMENT WAREHOUSE
www.lowes.com

LRH ENTERPRISES, INC.
www.lrhent.com

MAKITA
www.makita.com

METABO CORPORATION
www.metabo.com

MILWAUKEE ELECTRIC TOOL CORPORATION
www.mil-electric-tool.com

MINI MAX USA
www.minimax-usa.com

MLCS
www.mlcswoodworking.com

MOHAWK FINISHING PRODUCTS
www.mohawk-finishing.com

MURPHY-RODGERS, INC.
www.murphy-rodgers.com

ONEIDA AIR SYSTEMS
www.oneida-air.com

ONEWAY MANUFACTURING
www.oneway.ca

PANASONIC
www.panasonic.com

PASLODE
www.paslode.com

PAXTON WOODCRAFTERS' STORE
www.paxton-woodsource.com

PENN STATE INDUSTRIES
www.pennstateind.com

PLASTIC LUMBER COMPANY, INC.
www.plasticlumber.com

PORTER-CABLE CORPORATION
www.porter-cable.com

POWERMATIC
www.powermatic.com

PRO-TECH
www.protechpower.com

PS WOOD MACHINES
www.pswood.com

RARE EARTH HARDWOODS
www.rare-earth-hardwoods.com

RB INDUSTRIES, INC.
www.rbiwoodtools.com

RECORD TOOLS
www.recordtool.com

RIDGID WOODWORKING— EMERSON TOOL COMPANY
www.ridgidwoodworking.com

ROCKLER WOODWORKING SUPERSTORE
www.rockler.com

RYOBI
www.ryobi.com

SECO WOODWORKING MACHINERY — KUFO INDUSTRIES CORP.
www.seco-usa.com

SENCO
www.senco.com

SHOPSMITH, INC.
www.shopsmith.com

SIKKENS WOOD CARE PRODUCTS
www.sikkens.com

SIOUX TOOLS
www.siouxtools.com

SKIL POWER TOOLS
www.skil.com

STANLEY
www.stanleyworks.com

STAR MACHINE
www.starmachinery.com

SUNHILL MACHINERY
www.sunhillmachinery.com

TENRYU AMERICA, INC.
www.tenryu.com

TRADESMAN POWER TOOLS — POWER TOOL SPECIALISTS
www.tradesman-rexon.com

VAN DYKE'S RESTORERS
www.vandykes.com

VAUGHAN
www.vaughanmfg.com

WAGNER ELECTRONIC PRODUCTS, INC.
www.wwwagner.com

WILKE MACHINERY COMPANY
www.wilkemach.com

WOLFCRAFT, INC.
www.wolfcraft.com

WOOD CARVERS SUPPLY, INC.
www.woodcarverssupply.com

WOODCRAFT SUPPLY CORP.
www.woodcraft.com

WOODHAVEN, INC.
www.woodhaven.com

WOODTURNERS CATALOG
www.woodturnerscatalog.com

WOODWORKER'S HARDWARE
www.wwhardware.com

WOODWORKER'S SUPPLY, INC.
woodworker.com

WOODWORKER'S WAREHOUSE
www.woodworkerswarehouse.com

ZINSSER AND CO. INC.
www.zinsser.com

ASSOCIATIONS AND ORGANIZATIONS

AMERICAN ASSOCIATION OF WOODTURNERS
www.woodturner.org

AMERICAN FURNITURE MANUFACTURERS ASSOCIATION
www.afma4u.org

APA – THE ENGINEERED WOOD ASSOCIATION
www.apawood.org

ARTS & CRAFTS SOCIETY
www.arts-crafts.com

CALIFORNIA REDWOOD ASSOCIATION
www.calredwood.org

EARLY AMERICAN INDUSTRIES ASSOCIATION
www.eaiainfo.org

FURNITURE SOCIETY
www.furnituresociety.org

HAND TOOLS INSTITUTE
www.hti.org

HARDWOOD MANUFACTURERS ASSOCIATION
www.hardwood.org

HUMBOLDT WOODWORKERS GUILD
www.woodguild.com

INTERNATIONAL BUREAU OF WEIGHTS AND MEASURES
www.bipm.org

INTERNATIONAL WOOD COLLECTORS SOCIETY
www.woodcollectors.org

MID-WEST TOOL COLLECTORS ASSOCIATION
www.mwtca.org

NATIONAL HARDWOOD LUMBER ASSOCIATION
www.natlhardwood.org

NATIONAL INSTITUTE OF STANDARDS AND TECHNOLOGY
www.nist.gov

NATIONAL WOOD CARVERS ASSOCIATION
www.chipchats.org

OCCUPATIONAL SAFETY & HEALTH ADMINISTRATION
www.osha.gov

SOCIETY OF AMERICAN PERIOD FURNITURE MAKERS
www.sapfm.org

WOODLANDERS
www.woodlanders.com

WOODWORKING MACHINERY INDUSTRY ASSOCIATION
www.wmia.org

DESTINATIONS

CRAFTSMAN FARMS — THE GUSTAV STICKLEY MUSEUM
www.parsippany.net/craftsmanfarms.html

HENRY FORD MUSEUM & GREENFIELD VILLAGE
www.hfmgv.org

PUBLIC MUSEUM OF GRAND RAPIDS
www.grmuseum.org

SHAKER HISTORICAL MUSEUM
www.ohiohistory.org/places/shaker

VICTORIA AND ALBERT MUSEUM
www.vam.ac.uk

GENERAL INFO AND EDUCATION

AMERICAN SYCAMORE WOODWORKERS RETREAT
www.americansycamoreretreat.com

APPALACHIAN CENTER FOR CRAFTS
plato.ess.tntech.edu/acc

ARROWMONT SCHOOL OF ARTS & CRAFTS
www.arrowmont.org

CENTER FOR FURNITURE CRAFTSMANSHIP
www.woodschool.com

CHIPPENDALE INTERNATIONAL SCHOOL OF FURNITURE
www.chippendale.co.uk

COUNTRY WORKSHOPS WOODWORKING SCHOOL
www.countryworkshops.org

FOREST PRODUCTS LABORATORY, UNITED STATES DEPARTMENT OF AGRICULTURE, FOREST SERVICE
www.fpl.fs.fed.us

FOREST WORLD
www.forestworld.com

IOWA STATE UNIVERSITY DEPARTMENT OF FORESTRY
www.ag.iastate.edu/departments/forestry/Forestry.html

J.D. LOHR SCHOOL OF WOODWORKING
www.jdlohrwood.com/services.htm

JOHN C. CAMPBELL FOLK SCHOOL
www.folkschool.org

KENDALL COLLEGE OF ART AND DESIGN
www.kcad.edu

MARC ADAMS SCHOOL OF WOODWORKING
www.marcadams.com

MICHIGAN STATE UNIVERSITY FORESTRY DEPARTMENT
www.for.msu.edu

NORTH CAROLINA STATE UNIVERSITY ARTS PROGRAM
www.fis.ncsu.edu/arts

NORTHERN MICHIGAN UNIVERSITY DEPARTMENT OF ART AND DESIGN
www.nmu.edu/departments/art.htm

OREGON DEPARTMENT OF FORESTRY
www.odf.state.or.us

PENLAND SCHOOL OF CRAFTS
www.penland.org

ROCKINGHAM COMMUNITY COLLEGE
www.rcc.cc.nc.us

UNITED KINGDOM INSTITUTE FOR CONSERVATION OF HISTORIC AND ARTISTIC WORKS
www.ukic.org.uk

UNIVERSITY OF KENTUCKY DEPARTMENT OF FORESTRY
www.uky.edu/agriculture/forestry/forestry.html

UNIVERSITY OF MASSACHUSETTS DARTMOUTH COLLEGE OF VISUAL AND PERFORMING ARTS
www.umassd.edu/cvpa/wood.html

VIRGINIA DEPARTMENT OF FORESTRY
state.vipnet.org/dof/

VIRGINIA TECH DEPARTMENT OF FORESTRY
www.cnr.vt.edu/forestry/wwwmain.html

WOMEN IN WOODWORKING, ROCKLER
www.womeninwoodworking.com

WOOD FINISHING TECHNOLOGY PROGRAM OF DAKOTA COUNTY TECHNICAL COLLEGE
www.woodfinishing.org

WOODWORKER ACADEMY
www.woodworkeracademy.com

WOODWORKING FORUM, TIPS, ADVICE, SHOPPING
www.woodworking.com

WOODWORKING ON-LINE RESOURCE
www.woodzone.com

WOODWORKING SOFTWARE AND REFERENCE INFO
www.woodbin.com

GLOSSARY OF **woodworking words and phrases**

A

ACRYLIC RESIN: Invented in 1936, a thermoplastic used as an adhesive; also an ingredient in water-based paints and stains. Are transparent or pigmented.

ADHESIVE: A substance that holds materials together by surface attachment. It's a general term that includes a variety of substances, including cement, mucilage, paste and glue.

ADHESIVE JOINT: The location at which two adherends are held together with a layer of adhesive.

AMERICAN LUMBER STANDARD: This establishes standard sizes and requirements for the development and coordination of lumber grades of various species, and the implementation of those standards through an accreditation and certification program, set by the American Softwood Lumber Standard.

ASSEMBLY JOINT: Joints between variously shaped parts or subassemblies in wood furniture.

B

BACK-PRIMING: Applying a coat of primer to the back of a cabinet door panel to prevent warping.

BASTARD-SAWN: Primarily hardwood lumber in which the annual rings make angles of 30° to 60° with the surface of the piece.

BATTEN: A thin, narrow strip of (usually) plywood that conceals a joint between adjoining pieces of lumber or plywood.

BEVEL: A cut that is not 90° to a board's face, or the facet left by such a cut.

BIRD'S-EYE: Small, localized areas in wood with the fibers indented and contorted to form circular or elliptical figures on the surface; often found in sugar maple.

BISCUIT: A thin, flat oval of compressed beech that is inserted between two pieces of wood into mating saw kerfs made by a biscuit or plate joining machine.

BOARD: Lumber that is less than 38mm standard (2" nominal) thickness and greater than 38mm standard (2" nominal) in width. Boards less than 140mm standard (6" nominal) are sometimes called strips.

BOARD FOOT: A unit of measurement of lumber represented by a board that is 12" long, 12" wide and 1" thick, or the cubic equivalent of those measurements.

BOND: Basically, to glue together; veneers are "bonded" to create a sheet of plywood.

BOW: Distortion of a structural wood panel so that it is not flat lengthwise.

BRIDLE JOINT: A joint that combines features of both lap joints and mortise-and-tenon joints. It has a U-shaped mortise in the end of the board.

BURL: The hard, woody outgrowth on a tree, often used for highly figured, decorative veneers.

BUTT JOINT: The joint formed when two parts are fastened together without overlapping.

C

CARPENTER'S GLUE: White and yellow adhesives formulated for use with wood.

CASING: The trim framing a window, door or other opening.

CAULK: Waterproof sealant used to fill joints or seams; available as putty, a rope or a compound squeezed from a cartridge.

CHALK LINE: Line made by snapping a chalk-coated string against a plane.

CHAMFER: The flat surface created by slicing off the square edge or corner of a piece of wood or a panel.

CHECK: A separation between growth rings at the end of a board. Checks are common and lessen appearance, but do not weaken wood unless deep.

CHIPBOARD: A paperboard with a variety of uses.

CLEAVAGE: The separation in a joint caused by a wedge in an adhesively bonded joint.

CLOSE-GRAINED WOOD: Wood with narrow, inconspicuous annual rings; often designates wood with small pores.

COARSE-GRAINED WOOD: Wood with wide, conspicuous annual rings; often designates wood with large pores.

COLD-PRESSED PLYWOOD: Interior-type plywood manufactured in a press without external heat applied.

COMPOSITE PANEL: A veneer-faced panel with a reconstituted wood core.

COMPOUND MITER: A cut where the blade path is not perpendicular to the wood's end or edge and the blade tilt is not 90° to the face.

COOPERAGE: Containers consisting of two round heads and a body composed of staves held together with hoops, such as barrels or kegs.

COPING: Sawing a negative profile in one piece to fit the positive profile of another, usually in moulding.

CORBEL: A projection from the face of a wall or column supporting a weight.

CORE: The inner ply (or plies) whose grain runs perpendicular to that of the outer plies; or, a layer of reconstituted wood.

COUNTERBORE: A straight-sided drilled hole that recesses a screw head below the wood surface so a wood plug can cover it, or the bit that makes this hole.

COUNTERSINK: A cone-shaped drilled hole whose slope angle matches the underside of a flat screw head and sinks it flush with the wood surface, or the tool that makes this hole.

CROOK: An end-to-end warp along the board edge. Fit for horizontal.

CROSSBAND: The veneer layers with grain direction perpendicular to that of the face plies in plywood.

CROSSCUTTING: Sawing wood across the grain. Because the wood in structural wood panels is either cross-laminated or randomly oriented, any cut made in a structural wood panel is a crosscut. Always use a crosscut saw when hand or power sawing structural wood panels.

CROSS-GRAINED WOOD: Wood in which the fibers deviate from a line parallel to the sides of the piece.

CUP: Crosswise distortion from the flat plane of a structural wood panel.

CURLY-GRAINED WOOD: Wood in which the fibers are distorted so they have a curled appearance, as in bird's-eye maple.

D

DADO JOINT: Joint formed by the intersection of two boards, one of which is notched with a rectangular groove.

DECAY: The decomposition of wood caused by fungi.

DECORATIVE PANEL: An interior or exterior plywood panel grade with rough-sawn, brushed, grooved or striated faces.

DELAMINATION: The separation of layers in laminated wood or plywood due to adhesive failure.

DENSITY: Weight per unit volume. Density of wood is influenced by the rate of growth and the percentage of late wood.

DIAGONAL-GRAINED WOOD: Wood in which the annual rings are at an angle with the axis of the piece as a result of a swing at an angle with the bark of the tree.

DIMENSION: Lumber with a thickness from 38mm standard (2" nominal) up to, but not including, 114mm standard (5" nominal) and a width of greater than 38mm standard (2" nominal).

DOVETAIL JOINT: A traditional joint characterized by interlocking fingers and pockets shaped like its name. It has exceptional resistance to tension.

DOWEL: A small cylinder of wood that is used to reinforce a wood joint.

DRESSED SIZE: Dimensions of lumber after being surfaced with a planing machine, usually $1/2$" to $3/4$" less than the nominal (or rough) size.

DRESSING: The process of turning rough lumber into a smooth board with flat, parallel faces and straight, parallel edges and whose edges are square to the face.

DRY ROT: This term refers to any dry, crumbly wood rot, which usually causes the wood to become powdery.

E

EDGE-GRAINED LUMBER: Wood that has been sawed so the wide surfaces extend at about right angles to the annual growth rings.

EDGE JOINT: Joint made by bonding two pieces of wood together edge to edge, usually with glue; may be made by gluing two squared edges or by machined joints such as tongue-and-groove joints.

EDGE LAP: A notch into the edge of a board halfway across its width that forms half of an edge lap joint.

END GRAIN: The end of a piece of wood exposed when the wood fibers are cut across the grain, at right angles to the direction of the fibers.

END JOINT: Joint made by bonding two pieces of wood together end to end, often by a finger or scarf joint.

EXTERIOR PLYWOOD: Plywood bonded with an adhesive that is resistant to the effects of weather.

EXTRUDED PARTICLEBOARD: Particleboard made by shoving particles into a heated die, forming a rigid mass.

F

FACE: The highest-grade side of any veneer-faced panel that has outer plies of different veneer grades.

FASCIA: Wood or plywood trim used along the eave or the gable end of a structure.

FIBERBOARD: Sheet materials of a variety of densities that are manufactured from refined or partially refined wood fibers.

FIDDLEBACK-GRAINED WOOD: Often used for violin backs, this wood figure is produced by a type of fine, wavy grain found in maple and other wood species.

FIGURE: The pattern produced in a wood surface by annual growth rings, rays, knots or deviations from regular grain.

FINGER JOINT: End joint made up of several meshing wedges or fingers of wood bonded together with adhesive.

FINGERLAP: This specific joint of the lap family has straight, interwoven fingers; also called a box joint.

FINISH: Varnish, stain, paint, or any mixture that protects a surface; also refers to fine woodwork needed to complete a project, especially a building's interior.

FLAKEBOARD: Particle panel product composed of wood flakes.

FLAT-SAWN: The most common cut of lumber, where the growth rings run predominantly across the end of the board; or its characteristic grain pattern.

FLUSH: Level with an adjoining surface.

FOAM CORE: Center of a plywood "sandwich" panel. Liquid plastic foamed into all spaces between the plywood panels insulates and supports the component skins.

G

GLUE: Now synonymous with "adhesive," glue originally referred to a hard gelatin made of hides, tendons, cartilage, bones and other animal parts, and the adhesive created from this substance by heating it with water.

GLUE LINE: The adhesive joint formed between veneers in a plywood panel or between face veneers and core in a composite panel.

GRAIN: The natural growth pattern in wood. The grain runs lengthwise in the tree and is strongest in that direction.

GRAIN PATTERN: The visual appearance of wood grain. Types of grain pattern include flat, straight, curly, quilted, rowed, mottled, crotch, cathedral, bee's-wing, or bird's-eye.

GROUP NUMBER: Plywood is manufactured from over 70 species of softwood that are classified according to strength and stiffness into Groups 1 through 5. Group 1 woods are the strongest. The group number of a particular panel is determined by the weakest (highest numbered) species used in face and back (except for some thin panels where strength parallel to face grain is unimportant).

GROWTH RING: A tree's annual cross-sectional growth layer, including springwood and summerwood.

GUM: A sticky accumulation of resin that bleeds through finishes.

H

HARDBOARD: Panel manufactured from mostly wood, consolidated under heat.

HARDWOOD: Wood of the deciduous or broad-leaved trees — such as oak, maple, ash or walnut. *Hardwood* is only a general term, not a reference to actual wood hardness.

HEARTWOOD: The nonactive core of a tree distinguishable from the growing sapwood by its usually darker color and greater resistance to rot and decay.

I

INTERIOR PLYWOOD: Plywood manufactured for indoor use.

INTERLOCKED GRAIN: Grain in which the tree's wood fibers may slope in a right-handed direction for several years, then reverses to a left-handed direction for several years, and so on.

J

JIG: A shop-made or aftermarket device that assists in positioning and steadying the wood or tools.

JOINTING: The process of making a board face straight and flat or an edge straight, whether by hand or machine.

K

KERF: A slot made by a saw, or the width of a saw cut.

KEY: An inserted joint-locking device, usually made of wood.

KILN-DRIED: Wood dried in ovens, or kilns, by controlled heat and humidity to specified limits of moisture content. Veneers are kiln dried before the layup process.

KNIFE MARKS: The imprints or markings of the machine knives on the surface of dressed lumber.

KNOCKDOWN JOINT: A joint that is assembled without glue and can be disassembled and reassembled if necessary.

KNOT: Natural growth characteristic of wood caused by a branch base imbedded in the tree trunk.

KNOTHOLE: The void that is produced when a knot drops out of veneer.

L

LAMINATED VENEER LUMBER (LVL): Structural wood elements constructed of veneers laminated together with their fibers oriented in a parallel direction.

LAP: To position adjacent objects so that one surface extends over the other.

LAP JOINT: Joint made by placing one member partly over another and bonding the overlapped portions.

LENGTH JOINT: A joint that makes one longer wood unit out of two shorter ones by joining them end to end.

LEVEL: Absolutely horizontal.

LUMBER: The wood product of a sawmill and/or planing mill, with all four sides sawn and/or planed.

LUMBER CORE: Plywood manufactured with a core composed of lumber strips. The face and back, or outer, plies are veneer.

M

MACHINE BURN: Blunt planer knives may burn the face of the board.

MACHINE WAVE: Incorrect planer speeds may create waves on the face of the wood. Boards with waves must be thinned again.

MEDIUM-DENSITY FIBERBOARD (MDF): Panel product manufactured mostly from wood fibers combined with synthetic resin or other binding agents.

MEDIUM-DENSITY OVERLAY: Exterior-type plywood finished with an opaque resin-treated fiber overlay to provide a smooth surface ideal as a paint base. Recommended for siding and other outdoor applications, as well as for built-ins and furniture.

MILLING: The process of removing material to leave a desired positive or negative profile in the wood.

MITER: A generic term mainly meaning an angled cut across the face grain; or specifically a 45° cut across the face, end grain, or along the grain. See also bevel.

MORTISE: The commonly rectangular or round pocket into which a mating tenon is inserted. Mortises can be blind (stop inside the wood thickness), through, or open on one end.

MOULDING: A wood strip that has a curved or projected surface, used for decorative purposes.

N

NOMINAL SIZE: As applied to lumber, the size by which it is known and sold in the market, which often differs from the actual size.

O

ORIENTED STRAND BOARD (OSB): Particle panel product composed of strandlike flakes purposefully aligned in directions to make a panel stronger and stiffer.

OVERLAY: A thin layer of paper, plastic, film, metal foil or other material bonded to one or both faces of a piece of lumber or panel product to provide a protective or decorative face or a base for painting.

P

PALLET: A low wood or metal platform on which material can be stacked to facilitate mechanical handling, moving or storage.

PAPERBOARD: A substance that is thicker than paper, heavier and more rigid.

PARTICLEBOARD: A panel made of wood particles and glue.

PEELER LOG: A specially selected softwood log used to produce veneer.

PILOT HOLE: A small, drilled hole used as a guide and pressure relief for screw insertion, or to locate additional drilling work like countersinking and counterboring.

PITCH POCKETS: Pitch-filled spaces between grain layers. May bleed after board is milled; occasionally bleeds through finishes.

PITH FLECKS: Irregular, discolored streaks of tissue in wood, due to insect attacks on the growing tree.

PLY: A single veneer in a panel.

PLYWOOD: Panel made by laminating layers of wood.

PRESSURE-PRESERVATIVE TREATED: Wood treated with preservatives or fire retardants; treating solutions are pressure-injected into wood cells.

PRIMER: An undercoat applied to bare wood as a sealer and base for paint.

Q

QUARTER-SAWN: A stable lumber cut where the growth rings on the board's end run more vertically across the end than horizontally and the grain on the face looks straight; also called straight-grained or riftsawn.

R

RABBET JOINT: A joint formed by cutting a groove into the surface or along the edge of a board, plank or panel to receive another piece.

RAIL: A horizontal part of a frame.

> GLOSSARY OF WOODWORKING WORDS AND PHRASES CONTINUED

RAISED GRAIN: A roughened condition of the surface of dressed lumber in which the hard summerwood is raised above the softer springwood, but not torn loose from it.

RESAWN LUMBER: The product of sawing any thickness of lumber to develop thinner lumber.

RIPPING: Sawing wood in the direction of the grain.

ROUGH LUMBER: Lumber that has not been dressed or surfaced, but has been sawed, edged and trimmed.

S

SAPWOOD: The living wood of a tree, often an off-white, pale color, located near the outside of a log, outside the heartwood. Usually, sapwood is more susceptible to decay than heartwood.

SCARF JOINT: An angled or beveled end joint splicing pieces together.

SCRIBE: To make layout lines or index marks using a knife or awl.

SEASONING: Evaporation or extraction of moisture from green or partially dried wood.

SHAKE: A separation between growth rings that results in a slat coming loose from the face of the board.

SHIPLAP: Jointing in which ends or edges are notch-milled to overlap and form a rabbet joint.

SHOULDER: The perpendicular face of a step cut, like a rabbet, that bears against a mating joint part to stabilize the joint.

SLOPE OF GRAIN: The deviation of the line of fibers from a straight line parallel to the sides of the piece.

SOFTWOOD: Wood of the coniferous or needle-leaved trees — such as pine, fir, spruce or hemlock. *Softwood* is only a term, not a general reference to actual wood hardness.

SPLINE: A flat, thin strip of wood that fits into mating grooves between two parts to reinforce the joint between them.

SPRINGWOOD: The portion of the annual ring formed during the early part of the yearly growth period of a tree. Lighter in color, less dense and not as strong as summerwood.

STAIN: A pigment or dye used to color wood through saturation; or, a discoloration in wood from fungus or chemicals.

STEAM-BENDING: The process of forming curved wood members by steaming or boiling the wood and bending it to a form.

STILE: A vertical part of a door frame.

SUMMERWOOD: The portion of the annual ring formed during the latter part of the yearly growth of a tree. Darker in color, more dense and stronger than springwood.

SURFACED LUMBER: Lumber that has been dressed by running it through a planer.

T

TENON: The male part of a mortise-and-tenon joint, commonly rectangular or round; projects as the wood is cut away around it so it can be inserted into a mortise.

TEXTURE: Determined by relative size and distribution of the wood elements. Described as coarse (large elements), fine (small elements) or even (uniform size of elements).

TONGUE-AND-GROOVE JOINT: A system of jointing in which the rib or tongue of one member fits exactly into the groove of another.

TRIM: To crosscut a piece to any given length.

TWIST: A lopsided or uneven warp. Wood is weakened, but twisted boards are fit for non-load-bearing use.

V

VENEER: A thin sheet of wood laminated with others under heat and pressure to form plywood, or used for faces of composite panels. Also referred to as "ply."

W

WAFERBOARD: Panels manufactured from reconstituted wood wafers, as opposed to strands, bonded with resins under heat and pressure like oriented strand board (OSB).

WARP: The distortion in lumber that causes a departure from its original plane, usually developed during drying. Warp includes cupping, bowing, crooking and twisting.

WEIGHT: The weight of dry wood depends upon the cellular space, the proportion of wood substance to air space.

WIDTH JOINT: A joint that makes a unit of the parts by joining them edge to edge to increase the overall width of wood.

WOOD-BASED COMPOSITE PANEL: Generic term referring to material manufactured from wood veneer, strands, flakes, particles or fibers mixed with a synthetic resin or other bonding agent.

index

THE BEST WOODWORKING PROJECTS
COME FROM POPULAR WOODWORKING BOOKS!

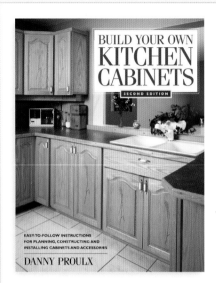

Plan, design, construct and install your own complete handmade kitchen, from simple cabinets and over-sink cupboards to lazy-Susan shelving, stemware storage and more. These start-to-finish guidelines make it easy. You'll also find practical information on kitchen design, material selection and tool shortcuts.

ISBN 1-55870-676-3, paperback,
128 pages, #70626-K

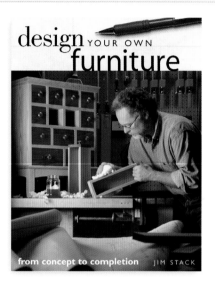

From beds to bookcases, this book provides all the instruction, advice and photos you need to master furniture design techniques with confidence. Jim Stack details everything from roughing out your initial concept to creating an accurate cutting list. You'll learn how to determine which design elements, materials and joinery techniques are right for the piece you have in mind.

ISBN 1-55870-613-5, paperback,
128 pages, #70555-K

Transform your underutilized corners and closets into valuable storage areas! It's easy once you know how. Rick Williams provides step-by-step instructions and full-color photos for 10 innovative projects that make the most of every valuable space. Each piece is beautiful and functional, with clever drawers and cabinets built right into the design.

ISBN 1-55870-594-5, paperback,
128 pages, #70534-K

Turn your woodshop scrap lumber into simple, inexpensive pieces of furniture that are both sturdy and attractive. These 15 intriguing projects include a wide variety of tables, a bedspread valet, a desk, a mirror frame and more. Author and woodworker Armand Sussman's project assembly methods are unique, using only a few saw cuts and glue.

ISBN 1-55870-543-0, paperback,
128 pages, #70404-K